HISTORIC PLACES OF OUR REPUBLIC

A Guide to Teaching United States History
for K-5 Elementary School Teachers and Parents

HISTORIC PLACES OF OUR REPUBLIC

A Guide to Teaching United States History
for K-5 Elementary School Teachers and Parents

KEN SCOVILLE

© 2017 by Ken Scoville

All rights reserved. This book, or parts thereof, may not be reproduced in any form or by any means, electronic or mechanical, without the expressed permission of the author.

Interior book design by Richard Fenwick at Good Looking Books

Cover design © 2017 by Lori Lieber Graphic Design, Inc.

Indexing by Nan Badgett

ISBN: 978-1-5336-4381-0

This book is dedicated to the National Park Service

HISTORIC PLACES OF OUR REPUBLIC

A Guide to Teaching United States History
for K-5 Elementary School Teachers and Parents

Introduction 1

About This Guide 5

Chapter 1: "Well Begun is Half Done" 11

Chapter 2: A Capital Perspective 33

Chapter 3: Curriculum and Standards 61

Chapter 4: Guiding Framework and
California Content Standards for Social Studies,
Kindergarten Through Second Grade....................................89

Chapter 5: Guiding Framework and
California Content Standards for Social Studies,
Third Through Fifth Grade 119

Chapter 6: All History is Local 145

Chapter 7: The Big Question: Why is the United States
the Nation it is Today? 165

Conclusion 185

References 189

Resources (Groups A-E) 191

Index...213

Acknowledgements 221

About the Author...223

Introduction

Imagine taking your students or children during their elementary school years to the National Mall in Washington, D.C., and other historic places throughout the United States. Here they could learn the history of our Republic, our representative democracy. These young historians could actually see these places and map their locations in relation to their own homes. Then they would read, write, and talk about the people, the decisions, and the actions that occurred at these places. The students would discover how the geography of these places contributed to what happened there. Each student could then write in a travelogue about what they learned by visiting these historic places. These new historians could discover why the United States is the nation it is today and see how the past impacts the present and future. Thanks to 21st century technology like Google Earth and YouTube, your students or children can visit specific historic places in their own homes or classroom.

Imagine again if you had to read about an important place from the past but you didn't know where it was or what it looked like today. How interested would you be? This is the usual template for studying the past, history. Students are told to read the chapter and answer the questions at the end. Then they hear that there will be a test on Friday with multiple-choice questions and they will start the next chapter on Monday. If you were one of these students, would you see any purpose to learning (often just memorizing) this information? Would you think that these events in the past had any relationship to your life today? Would you be curious to discover more? All of your responses are likely to be "no."

This is too often the experience with history in middle and high school. Much of the elementary school experience related to social studies/history revolves around national holidays such as Presidents Day and Dr. Martin Luther King, Jr.'s birthday. While these are great opportunities, a meaningful and connected approach to United States history during a student's important foundational years of education is a rarity. This is the time to nurture the natural curiosity that children have about the world and where they live. Those of us, myself included, who traveled to different locations in the United States during childhood and saw historic places somehow kept our curiosity intact through less than inspirational classroom experiences. I still wanted to know more about the past because of interesting places I had seen and remembered from childhood vacations. I knew I wanted to see and experience these historic places as an adult and to seek out other "old" places.

In the most simple terms, the study of the past should begin with a historic place as it exists today that you can see via Google Earth, YouTube, and later in person. Then students can understand where it is located in relation to where they currently live. This personal relationship begins the development of a cognitive map of historic places to connect to the events that happened there. This study of the past is called "history" and is one of the social sciences. All of the social sciences attempt to understand human behavior. History is studying human behavior in the past while incorporating the other social sciences for greater understanding of this behavior. The history of human endeavor looks at people and their decisions and the resulting actions. Since we all live on the Earth (except for the pioneers in the International Space Station), the geography of a place usually impacts the decisions and actions taken there.

We live in the present and this dictates that the past must be discovered in the present. Such discovery begins the process of developing an awareness that the past is impacting the present and often the future. The most accessible way to understand this is to think about your home. The place each one of us calls "home" becomes a historic location of the history of our life. The sight of our home conjures up specific thoughts and emotions with the other senses reinforcing these responses. Our family and the events of growing up are organized and remembered with this place we call "home."

We vividly remember the location of our childhood home and where it is in relation to where we now live as adults. We know the decisions and actions that our family took while living there. There may have been a lake or hill nearby or even a favorite tree to climb as a child. The geography of where the house was located affected the events that happened there. It could be as simple as living close enough to school that you could walk home for lunch, or hanging out at a favorite place so long that you were often late for dinner. These events become memories that are connected to these places and are remembered in the present and the future. Whether we realize it or not, these past experiences, both good and bad, affect our lives in the present and often the future. We may decide that we want to live our lives in our childhood town, or we may move somewhere else to start a new life. Our home is the most personal example of a historic place for studying the past, the history of our life.

A gathering process to understand the past includes looking at many different items that were made at a specific time in the past. These are called "primary sources," and they include the historic places that vividly tell us about the people and their decisions and actions that occurred there, as well as the impact of geography on all of this. Most importantly, we need to look at why certain events in the past happened, as best we can determine in the present, and how these events impact our life today. This is the experience that children should have as they learn the history of the nation that we call home, the United States of America.

Every year of elementary school, students will visit the National Mall in Washington, D.C. This visual discovery of our representative democracy introduces the structures of our Republic and that citizens are the government. We elect fellow citizens to represent us at all levels of government – federal, state, and local. These visits provide the foundation for further civic education and the ongoing responsibilities of citizens in our Republic.

The chapters in this guide will lead you to an organizing framework that you can use for this endeavor. I will use scholarly advice and content standards that influence classroom instruction in social studies/history. Included are key historic places, starting with the National Mall, online resources, and supplemental reading suggestions. I will attempt to simplify and prioritize when possible a curriculum based on this guiding framework that will be adaptable for elementary school teachers and parents. This guide is also applicable in the field when visiting historic places with your children or students, especially the National Mall in Washington, D.C.

I am your guide in the present to explore the past of the United States so that in the future you can be a guide for your students in the classroom or your children at home.

About This Guide

Chapter 1

Learning is productive only with an organized, purposeful approach. To create such an approach, this chapter emphasizes the development of a guiding framework. There are six categories divided into two groups; the first three deal with preparing for the study of the past/history, while the second three deal with the actual study of the past/history. All six categories connect for successful instruction, and each category is supported and clarified with scholarly perspectives.

The guiding framework provides the structure for successful instruction no matter your level of knowledge of United States history.

Chapter 2

Where to begin our study of United States history is a major focus for the chapter. The Capitol in Washington, D. C., and the National Mall specifically, is the logical beginning. You will be taken through each step of the guiding framework and will use Google Earth and YouTube to visit the Mall and the Washington Monument to understand the use of the framework. An introduction of the foundational knowledge that applies under each category of the framework will also be indicated.

Chapter 3

The development of curriculum and the use of standards is discussed in a straightforward manner with definitions of specific terms. The importance of following a defined curriculum throughout elementary school is emphasized. A narrative that includes the guiding framework and the specifics of the foundational knowledge for United States history at each grade level is presented in detail.

Chapter 4

Here the guiding framework is presented with indicated work under each category within the context of specific state standards. This assembles the standards, guiding framework, and the work to be accomplished for each grade. This becomes the curriculum to develop a foundational knowledge of United States history and the indicated standards. Kindergarten through second grade is the focus in this chapter and the work covers an entire school year.

Chapter 5

The curriculum continues, containing the guiding framework and the work to be accomplished for each grade level to obtain a foundational knowledge of United States history and the indicated standards. Now third grade through fifth grade is the focus; again, this work covers an entire school year.

Chapter 6

The use of local history to teach national history is the focus for this chapter. There are many opportunities to use local and regional sources to understand what was happening throughout the nation at specific times in our nation's past. The introduction of eras in our history and how local and regional resources and historic places tell the story of our national history is organized with examples. There are opportunities to use local history for all grade levels, and especially in fourth grade, where the emphasis is on state history with most content standards throughout the nation.

Chapter 7

The guiding framework and the work that students accomplish during their elementary school career has prepared them to answer the question, "Why is the United States the nation it is today?" A return tour of the National Mall, monuments and memorials, the three branches of our representative democracy, the National Archives, Library of Congress, and Smithsonian Museums provides the answer. The importance of the words in our founding documents is emphasized. In addition, this chapter introduces two timeless debates: How much should government be involved in our lives and at what level? The second debate concerns citizenship. Who should have the rights of citizenship, and what are the specifics of those rights?

References
Resources (Groups A through E)
Index

There is nothing so American as our national parks . . . The fundamental idea behind the parks . . . is that the country belongs to the people . . .

~ President Franklin Delano Roosevelt, 1936

The idea of preserving in a national grouping such spots of scenic beauty and historic memory originated here in this country . . . In Europe, Asia, Africa, and Latin America, other countries have followed our pioneering example and set aside their most magnificent scenic areas as national treasures for the enjoyment of present and future generations.

~ President Dwight D. Eisenhower, 1963

Our National Parks belong to each of us, and they are natural places to learn, exercise, volunteer, spend time with family and friends, and enjoy the magnificent beauty of our great land.

~ President George W. Bush, 2008

Chapter 1

"Well Begun is Half Done"

This quote is credited to Aristotle and I like to think he was thinking of students just beginning school. When children begin their quest for learning, whether at home or in a formal school setting, they are very curious about the world. Their senses need new experiences with music, pictures, and objects to touch and smell. These sensory experiences are the gateway to language development and resulting vocabulary. The outdoors is beckoning with experiences that reinforce curiosity. A good beginning for your role as a guide is responding to this curiosity in an organized manner.

So much of teaching is about sequencing a lesson, and if it is not done in an organized manner, curiosity is diminished and sometimes even lost. Most of us are visual learners and seeing an image of where you are going comes first, followed by the geographic location and geographic features, and finally by written and spoken words about this place and location. A simple walk around the school campus or your neighborhood begins with a Google Earth visit to understand the layout of your home or school buildings and landscape in the context of your surrounding community. The Google Earth image of this view is taken on the walk as students begin their observations and record them in a travelogue in the field. An awareness of where the Sun is on this stroll begins the understanding of directions, along with noting on the picture where north, south, east, and west are. Back at home or the classroom, a discussion of the observations and asking the students to indicate where this observation was made is important. Identifying words that need to be defined and encouraging students to write to the best of their ability about their observations completes this organized field trip.

Too often in school children are confined to the classroom for learning without any reinforcement from outside. Many elementary schools try to get students off campus to see more of the world but either from budgets or testing issues, the field trip becomes a casualty.

As your guide in the present to explore the past, this structure of seeing the place via technology first, even if you are going to visit in person, is essential. Understanding the geographic location related to where you are currently is next, followed by the gathering of knowledge about this place. History is an abstract endeavor and requires all three elements to become meaningful and be retained in one's memory. The place and its location are critical for retaining and valuing the information about the place. As adults, many of our clearest memories of our elementary school come from the field trips. I can still remember going to the airport in Phoenix, Arizona, as part of an elementary school field trip. Two vivid aspects of that trip were the control tower and getting on an airplane; the interior rake of the plane was so steep that I was curious enough to later find out that the plane was a DC-3. Anytime I return to Phoenix and pass Sky Harbor Airport, I always think of this field trip.

I spoke about the necessity of being organized in our approach to teaching about the past and I have developed a guiding framework to accomplish this. This framework has two parts: The first part has three categories that deal with preparing for the study of the past, history, while the second part has three categories that deal with the actual study of the past, history. We all learn and retain information easily with groupings of three. This "rule of three" is used in many endeavors from public speaking to writing and advertising. A few great examples from the past are:

We hold these truths to be self-evident, that all men are created equal, that they are endowed by their creator with certain unalienable Rights, that among these are life, liberty and the pursuit of happiness. (Declaration of Independence)

. . . that from these honored dead we take increased devotion to that cause for which they gave the last full measure of devotion—that we here highly resolve that these dead shall not have died in vain—that this nation, under God, shall have a new birth of freedom—and that government of the people, by the people, for the people, shall not perish from the earth. (Gettysburg Address)

Never before in the field of human conflict was so much owed by so many to so few. (Sir Winston Churchill)

The guiding framework has this grouping structure so the elements can be retained more easily, but there is greater significance. The first three are the building blocks to make the next three successful. All six categories are based on my readings and experiences in researching and teaching United States history.

Another aspect of these six categories also relates to learning and retaining information. This is the idea of gestalt, "the whole is stronger than the individual parts." This concept evolves from a philosophy in the 1890s that was later used in psychology and I think it is most easily explained from a design perspective. When we look at a tile floor we acknowledge the floor in its entirety, but we don't immediately recognize each individual tile. What we see is the tile floor, the floor being a stronger image than the individual tiles. Similarly, the six categories in the guiding framework are an organized whole for the study of the past, history. Each category is important, but only in its entirety is it effective in the study of history.

The Six Categories of the Guiding Framework

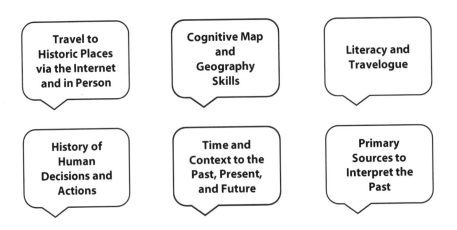

The top three concepts are the necessary preparation *to address the study of history*. The bottom three concepts are necessary *for the study of history*.

Travel to Historic Places via the Internet and in Person

> **Travel to Historic Places via the Internet and in Person**

The starting point for this guiding framework includes historic places in our country and their importance for understanding the past of the United States and the world. We need places to organize the reality of this study of the past, the history. Places are like libraries: They store all kinds of knowledge about the past with resources that include landscapes and structures or remains that can be centuries old. Preserving these places in a manner that reflects the past is counter to much of our current life, but individuals and organizations have accomplished a great deal to this end. The National Park Service preserves and interprets the greatest collection of historic places and landscapes of any organization in the world. They also preserve the artifacts and other resources that are part of these places.

I have been involved with historic preservation efforts in my own community for decades and I know it is important to understand what makes a place historic. The Secretary of the Interior has established guidelines for this designation and the National Park Service, which is part of the Department of the Interior, uses these guidelines. What makes a place historic usually includes one or more of the following features, according to the Department of the Interior: "There is an association with events that have made significant contributions to our history, are associated with significant persons in our past, and possess distinctive characteristics of design or construction with high artistic value of the time."[1] A significant amount of information

---

[1] np.gov/Nr/national_register_fundamentals.htm

is available online through the Department of the Interior site specifying how these features are identified so as to justify the preservation of a "historic" place. These qualities are the reason historic places are critical to our understanding and connection to the past/history. These preserved places from the past guide us as we make unique connections to our understanding of the history.

This preservation effort allows such a connection to be possible. The visitor to Independence Hall and other preserved places can experience what author James Marston Fitch, in his book *Historic Preservation: Curatorial Management of the Built World* (1990, pp. xi-xii), calls ". . . two interconnected faces of consciousness: direct sensuous perception ('I saw it with my own eyes') and intellectual cognition ('Everyone knows that this is where the Declaration of Independence was signed')." This experience is the strongest with an in-person visit, but technology like Google Earth allows us to make this connection and illustrates that these historic places still exist in the present.

Without this conservation effort by the National Park Service and other organizations, our understanding of the history of the United States would be severely limited. All these places are preserved for the citizens of our country to enjoy but, more importantly, to enable us to learn about our Republic and the responsibilities of citizenship. Historic places in our nation allow us to see and begin to understand the decisions and actions that led to and have preserved our Republic. Connecting students to these places and to the history that transpired can begin to fulfill a critical mission of education in the United States.

> Since this country was founded it has been understood that teachers and schools were critical to the nation's future . . . The reason that our eighteenth-century Founders and their nineteenth-century successors believed schools were crucial

to the American future was not only that the schools would make students technically competent. That aim was important, but their main worry was whether the Republic would survive at all. (*The Making of Americans: Democracy and our Schools*, E. D. Hirsch, Jr., 2009, p. 3)

The second category of this framework brings reality to the existence of these places from the past.

Cognitive Map and Geography Skills

> Cognitive Map
> and
> Geography
> Skills

The understanding of where a historic place is located based on your current location is the second category of the framework. Such understanding is a necessary component to connect the knowledge of what happened at this historic place. Geography is an integral aspect of place and is understood as it relates to the place itself and to the development of a cognitive map for each of us to locate this place. All aspects of geography are involved in defining a specific location and exploring the impact on the people who lived there. Mountains and rivers, forests and deserts, and their specific climates caused certain human actions relating to the use and value of the place or the justification to do battle to defend the location.

The land on which we live has always shaped us. It has shaped the wars, the powers, politics, and social development of the peoples that now inhabit nearly every part of the earth. Technology may seem to overcome the distances between us in both mental and physical space, but it is easy to forget that the land where we live, work, and raise our children is hugely important and that the choices of those who lead the seven billion inhabitants of this planet will to some degree always be shaped by the rivers, mountains, deserts, lakes, and seas that constrain all of us—as they always have. (*Prisoners of Geography*, Marshall, p. 1)

Everywhere we live today is intertwined with the geography of the place and the emotional sense that this is home, or it serves a specific need in our lives whether for employment or health, for example. We develop a cognitive map connected to the place we call home. The research is uncertain as to whether it is an actual map in our mind or a series of images that leads us in specific directions in the place we call home. But it is, in any case, a genuinely reliable map.

Cartographer Jerry Bretton in his book, *A History of the World in 12 Maps* (2012, p. 4), states, "From early childhood onwards, we make sense of ourselves in relation to the wider physical world by processing information spatially. Psychologists call this activity 'cognitive mapping,' the mental device by which individuals acquire, order and recall information about their spatial environment . . ."

This "map" takes us to work and shopping as well as to recreation and retreat. We organize information related to these locations such as where we park our car or a quicker way to get home in rush-hour traffic. This ability to map locations in our mind and organize information is critical to understanding the history of places and the human events that took place there. Bretton goes on to speak about an experience that we all have had multiple times in life, being lost. "The urge to map is a basic human instinct. Where would we be without maps? The obvious answer is, of course, 'lost'..." (Bretton, 2012, p. 4) Too often in teaching history as an experience in memorization, students get lost. Instruction in history should connect to historic places so that organization and understanding within a cognitive map is established. This can only happen with the development of geography skills that begin as simply as a walk around one's neighborhood or school campus. Again, this is accomplished in an organized manner.

All this discussion of cognition and perception really means just thinking. This is the way we acquire knowledge and understanding. As your guide, I want to provide scholarly perspectives and then simplify them so that you can guide your students.

Children learn where their home, school, sports field, movie theater, shopping center, and favorite restaurant are in their community. As they grow older and develop a cognitive map of all this and more, they continue to add more information specific to each location and eventually walk, bike, and drive to these locations. Students who approach the study of the past by seeing historic places in the present, indicating their location on an outline map of the United States, and then connecting with information, will retain this knowledge. As they do this over their time in elementary school, they will develop a cognitive map of historic places in the United States to which they can add more information throughout their school career and life.

Literacy and Travelogue

> **Literacy and Travelogue**

In order for students to connect information to these historic places, they need to become literate: This is the third category of the framework. The meaning of the word "literacy" is the ability to read and write and express one's knowledge. "To be culturally literate is to possess the basic information needed to thrive in the modern world. The breadth of that information is great, extending over the major domains of human activity from sports to science." (*Cultural Literacy: What Every American Needs to Know*, E. D. Hirsch, Jr., 2009, p. xiii)

This is what education is all about. Literacy begins with the meaning of words, and the development of vocabulary is a cornerstone for success in school and life. In my experiences of teaching and tutoring students, their not knowing what a word means or that meanings can change based on context is pervasive. Students think they know the meaning of a word but when they are asked directly, it is clear they are just guessing. It is imperative that students know the meanings of words and review the meanings by using the words in a sentence. This needs to be accomplished with both the spoken and written word.

I feel compelled to mention here an issue concerning the perspective of reading and literacy. In my years of advocating for history instruction in elementary schools, I have found that many teachers see time spent on instruction in history as a separate endeavor rather than time spent for reading. If certain topics are not taught in school, vocabulary and context for future reading experiences are missed. Reading in all subject areas and developing an understanding of the meanings of words based on a subject are essential to becoming literate.

Most human endeavors are constantly debated, and education and learning are topics of heated discussions. Certain theorists promoted learning as a natural process without a list of items that all children should know; others would take a narrow approach to what should be taught. For this guide, I align with the anthropological explanation for the education of children:

> The anthropological view stresses the universal fact that a human group must have effective communications to function effectively, that effective communications require shared culture, and that shared culture requires transmission of specific information to children. Literacy, an essential aim of education in the modern world, is no autonomous, empty skill but depends on a literate culture. Like any other aspect of acculturation, literacy requires the early and continued transmission of specific information . . . (Hirsch, 1990, p. xvii)

The early and ongoing effort this guide advocates in the instruction of United States history is the pathway for literacy about our representative democracy and past efforts to fulfill the ideals set by the Charters of Freedom (Declaration of Independence, United States Constitution, and the Bill of Rights). This ongoing instruction in elementary school provides the foundation of knowledge that guides students to our nation and the world of today.

Instruction in history/social studies always includes new vocabulary. This in turn begins the process of reading, writing, discussing, and developing positions about the past and present of the United States. This process is only possible with the other aspect of literacy which is the development of questions. I will look at questioning strategies and the Socratic Method in the next chapter.

The development of literacy needs to be seen by students as ongoing and valued. This is the reason for a travelogue where students will write new vocabulary words, questions, and answers generated from observations, readings and discussions. This travelogue will be accomplished with each lesson and will continue throughout the elementary school years. Geography work and research accomplished by students will also be included. Each year's travelogue should be retained for the students to have for the future. The travelogue will become an important component of their understanding of primary sources as they grow older.

IMPORTANT: This travelogue needs to be in a more permanent form such as a spiral notebook or even an electronic device; I prefer a paper format with an electronic copy. Students' work with geography skills and the cognitive map needs to be connected with the written work in the travelogue. This will be retained for the entire year and then scanned and saved. I have observed too many elementary school classrooms where students do this type of literacy work and then it quickly becomes lost, especially in the primary grades. Students need to be given the message that what they have written and mapped is important and that the progress they are making is visible. Their efforts also become a historical record that will be used later with the category of primary sources and valued by students when they reach adulthood. This will be a primary source of their learning in elementary school.

REMINDER: The introduction of the first part of the guiding framework is complete. These three categories (concept of three) prepare us for the study of the past/history.

The sequence is important with historic places as the start, then viewing these places with technology, and finally viewing in person, if possible. The second is the development of geography skills and a cognitive map. Students make and use maps to understand how geography has impacted the past and present. The cognitive map organizes information around the actual place where an event happened. The third is literacy in the form of a travelogue to record new vocabulary, readings, writing, and discussions to reinforce daily instruction and develop a permanent record of their progress. The travelogue and the cognitive map are connected and refer to the historic places.

The second part of this introduction includes three categories that deal with the actual study of the past/history.

History of Human Decisions and Actions

> **History of Human Decisions and Actions**

History, the study of the past, is one of the social sciences. I think there is continuing confusion as to whether teachers are giving instruction in history or social studies. Like all human endeavors, there are turf issues within education regarding emphasis on history or social studies. Currently, the emphasis is on social studies but the debate is ongoing. I consider myself a historian and, as your guide, I use social studies in the context of teaching history.

It may be helpful to think of social studies curriculum development over time as a negotiation, if not a war, among competing camps, each with its own leaders, philosophy, beliefs, and pedagogical practices. During the hundred-year-long conversation on the nature of social studies in schools, one camp emerges as prominent for a time, only to recede a few years later (*The Social Studies Wars: What Should We Teach Our Children?* Ronald W. Evans, 2004, p. 3)

Authors Hellstern, Scott, and Garrison, in their book, *The History Student Writer's Manual*, speak to the relationship of all these social sciences that are involved with studying the past:

In its primary goal, history is related to the other academic disciplines, such as economics, geography, philosophy, political science, psychology, and sociology. Sociologists, for example, study the way groups act. So do historians, only in the past tense. Psychologists explore the mysteries of the mind and of individual patterns of behavior. So do historians, in the past tense. Perhaps the subject matter or the approach to it changes from discipline to discipline, but each of them represents a different approach to the common goal of gaining a clearer, fuller understanding of the way human beings are... The objective is to discover why we do the things we do—what makes us tick. (1997, pp. 2-3)

The discipline of geography is of great impact in this historic place approach, both for understanding the decisions and actions that people took and to organize our study of the past with a cognitive map. When someone teaches history, they are in fact teaching social studies by the very endeavor of teaching history. For my purposes, I will indicate history when I am referencing instruction in history and using the other social sciences to understand the past, the history.

There are additional scholarly aspects to studying the past and historians have specific areas that they identify for their instruction of history. An aspect of all scholarship is the conflicting views and changes to an argument's validity over time. This is especially apparent in textbooks about the history of our country and the world. Every textbook adoption committee for a school district is aware of this and opinions come from every perspective.

> Part of the problem, I believe, is that many young people do not understand how history is researched and written about, nor do they see or understand the impact past decisions have on their lives today. Sadly, even fewer students have any concept that history is constantly being affected by individual historians as well as our society's own biases, prejudices, perspectives, and interpretations. (*History in the Making*, Kyle Ward, 2006, pp. xviii-xix)

I have chosen this specific scholarly resource from essays in the *Journal of American History* ("Teaching American History," Essays, Eds. Gary J. Kornblith and Carol Lasser, 2009) to get at the essence of the study of the past, history. I value an approach to the study of United States history for elementary school students that takes an elevated approach that can be simplified for this age group.

These editors distilled from these essays three key directions for study. The first is ". . . to recover the pastness of the past and to recognize the presentness of the past." The second deals with ". . . historical causation: contingency, with its emphasis on free will and individual agency, and determinism, with its emphasis on the role played by forces beyond individuals' control." The third deals with ". . . research in primary sources to locate evidence and establish historical facts and the need to construct historical interpretations in dialogue with other scholars because the facts do not 'speak for themselves'" (Kornblith and Lasser, 2009, pp. 2-3).

For simplicity I will define <u>the first</u> area as, the past is part of our present and future. <u>The second</u>, human history, is about people and their decisions and actions. There is a constant interplay of these decisions and actions taken with elements that stay in control versus those that spin out of control. The geography of the setting is usually a part of this interplay. Finally, <u>the third</u> area of focus is on primary and secondary sources with expert positions to construct arguments that answer the "why" questions in history.

Time and Context to the Past, Present, and Future

People like us who believe in physics know that the distinction between the past, the present and the future is only a stubbornly persistent illusion.

~ Albert Einstein

> **Time and Context to the Past, Present, and Future**

The past is an abstract concept. Of the three elements of time, the past does not seem to be very important because it appears to have no connection with the present or future. We all live in the moment and often look forward to the future. Even after living for a half century, the past is difficult to grasp, but we can acknowledge that for our own lives, the past certainly impacted our present and likely our future. This is not the case with children in elementary school whose teacher is informing the class that they will be studying past events in the United States and the world.

The next step in the formula will be asserting that studying the past is called "history" and people like George Washington lived a long time ago. Now the idea of time and what a year or decade or century means to a child of eight becomes an issue. This becomes more perplexing given that no one alive today ever met or spoke with the Father of our Country and there are no photographs of him. There are, however, paintings and sculptures of his face and books with the words that he wrote. To make some sense of George Washington and his continuing impact on our country, even as adults, we need to see the places where he lived, worked, and died. As I mentioned earlier, we live in the present and I believe that instruction about the past begins in the present. This is especially important for elementary schoolchildren. When students see a historic place like the White House via Google Earth and YouTube videos, it is real because it about their present. This is an opportunity to generate curiosity about the past, the present, and the future and the concept of time as best as can be understood for this age group and even for adults.

Author William A. Ward said, "Curiosity is the wick in the candle of learning." Curiosity is the great motivator for human endeavor. The diversity of human curiosity makes the world what it is today. But this great motivator only works with memory. If you couldn't remember, you would be like a car that was always idling and could never be driven. Curiosity provokes the desire to learn and then remember and connect to new learning. Very early in this process another issue comes into view. To understand the present, what has happened in the past must be sought out. It is possible to accept your reality based on the present but hopefully curiosity would intervene and demand that past endeavors need to be explored in order to understand the present. This is the pathway to begin to assess the future. "The past is part of our present and future" develops a perspective that builds on all future learning related to history. This way of thinking is essential to heighten curiosity and assign value to studying the past.

28 • Historic Places of our Republic

Primary Sources to Interpret the Past

> **Primary Sources to Interpret the Past**

At first glance, one might think that all the emphasis on technology and the future would make the study of the past seem less important or interesting. The development of Google Earth, YouTube, and a vast array of information on the Internet is a renaissance for the study of the past. This guidebook would be severely hampered without this new technology. In a very general way, primary sources are the array of manmade accomplishments during the period in the past that is being studied. The types of primary sources include written words of the time such as diaries, letters, and legal documents; clothing and practical items; paintings and photographs; musical recordings and motion pictures; artifacts from below the ground through archeological exploration; and buildings. Historic places, landscapes designed by man, and preserved natural areas can also be included. Secondary sources were written after the time being studied but use primary sources. Textbooks and biographies of people from the past are examples of secondary sources.

Secondary source material can play a critical role, especially for students, who usually do not know enough context to base their interpretations on primary sources alone. The importance of primary materials can be overstated. Such sources are not intrinsically more reliable than secondary sources; indeed, often they are less reliable. After all, the actors in an event have vested interests to portray their own actions positively. Historians coming along ten or a hundred years later may be much less biased. (*Teaching What Really Happened*, James W. Loewen, 2010, pp. 90-91)

The availability of primary sources online is overwhelming and thrilling at the same time. All our great libraries and museums with their vast collections can be accessed, with some restrictions about copies, for visual inspection and referenced for discussions and written work. Once-in-a-lifetime traveling collections can often be referenced online and visited in person. YouTube has so much in the way of documentary footage and current experiences at historic places and if you are interested, hours can go by. I encourage the use of YouTube and online web sites but in a balanced perspective so that reading, writing, and discussions are at the forefront. All of these sources, primary and secondary, are only a means to an end, not the end. This selection process also includes determining whether a source is credible.

We still have the census, newspaper archives, and many other sources, many of which, unlike the web, making them arguably more credible. Second, every source–from the web, the library or their textbook–needs to be annotated. The annotation–as short as a sentence or even a phrase–tells why this source is credible. (Loewen, 2010, p. 84)

These irreplaceable visual opportunities allow us to connect by seeing and hearing inspiring moments in our history. Dr. Martin Luther King, Jr.'s "I Have a Dream" speech during the March on Washington at the National Mall must be seen and heard but the words themselves need to be read and understood also. The resources preserved by the National Park Service, museums, archives, and other agencies will be explored and referenced in this guide.

Google Earth specifically allows students to visit the

landscapes and built environments that preserve the history of our country. "The application benefits and subsequent popularity are obvious to anyone who has used it. As well as drawing on the iconic image of the blue planet suspended in space popularized by NASA in the 1970s, Google Earth offers its users a level of interaction with the earth unimaginable on printed paper maps or atlases" (Brotton, 2012, p. 406). This 21st century technology captures the interest of young people and makes connections in a way never before available as learning experiences. Seeing these places online generates more curiosity and illustrates the spatial relationships from where one lives and where the preserved area is. The visual introduction in the present and the spatial relationship are always the first two steps in the sequence of learning, coming before the detailed written and spoken word. This is the structure that promotes organization and comprehension. All of these actions build a desire to actually visit these places to satisfy curiosity. For many of us, it will increase curiosity and our emotional connection to the United States and our opportunities as citizens.

The guiding framework provides the organization for this guide and addresses the unique requirements for a successful study of the past, history. The framework will be used in its entirety for every grade level but approached with the abilities of the age of the students in mind. Each year the expectations will build on the accomplishments of the past year; the topics and skill level will vary every year. Consistency in the use of the framework will allow students to gain a foundational knowledge of the history of the United States. This framework functions for teachers and parents who are, like all citizens of the United States, from diverse backgrounds with different levels of knowledge concerning the history of the country we live in.

Most of us have scattered pieces of knowledge concerning that history and would recognize names like George Washington and Abraham Lincoln, as well as documents like the Declaration of Independence and the Constitution. Hopefully, we know something about the accomplishments of these men and how the documents impacted the development of the United States. We know about a War for Independence and the War Between the States, along with world wars and possibly the Great Depression. The Martin Luther King, Jr. national holiday has brought a greater emphasis on the quest for "liberty and justice for all." The guiding framework provides the structure for successful instruction no matter your level of knowledge.

In addition to the variations in knowledge are the variations in backgrounds for teaching. This guide is also intended for parents who may have little knowledge about teaching but are highly motivated to work with their children concerning the history of our country and citizenship. Given these concerns, I will purposely be repetitive in the presentation of many of the topics and approaches that are discussed. Later in this guide I will also mention the instruction technique of "spiraling," a major approach of this guide that can often seem repetitive. I think that this approach is highly effective to bring students to the desired level they can reach by the end of their elementary school career.

If I posed the question, "Why is the United States the nation it is today?", answering the question would seem to be an overwhelming task. I think it is perfectly possible that a student completing fifth grade could answer this question in a meaningful way by using the approach this guide takes. This approach will develop and nurture a curiosity about the past through the use of the guiding framework and by what we can see and experience today, thanks to preservation efforts by the National Park Service and other private organizations involved in these same endeavors.

Twenty-first century technology, the social sciences and traditional literacy development are blended together in the sequence of the guiding framework. The next chapter will address the use of the framework with guidelines for the specific work at various grade levels. These guidelines promote the student's development of a foundational knowledge of the history of the United States to be successful in school and as a citizen of our nation. Now that we are organized in our approach, the next question is, where to begin?

Here is the guiding framework in its entirety, with the first group of three categories to *prepare for the study* of the past/history, while the second group has three categories to deal with the *actual study* of the past/history. Connected as they are here, you can see that all six categories function together in the teaching of history as one complete approach.

The Six Categories of the Guiding Framework

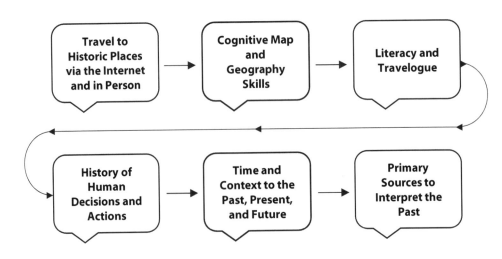

Chapter 2

A Capital Perspective

If you are an elementary school teacher, parent, or both, where to begin would be your first question for teaching the history of United States to your student. Usually, the start to teaching history is from a chronological perspective, beginning with the earliest times. In contrast, the present is the perspective taken in this guide. What exists today from the past is often given the status of being historic. Historic places exist all across the United States. The guiding framework that I explained in the first chapter is now put into practice to illustrate how to use each category and answer questions of how to proceed. There are six categories in the framework, with the first category being historic places. The capital of a nation includes many places that are historic and intertwined with the government of a nation. This is true with our capital in Washington, D.C. The first historic place to begin our study is the National Mall in our capital city.

The capital of the new United States of America would express the youth, exuberance, and boundless potential of a nation and its people. Moreover, as the seat of government it

34 • Historic Places of our Republic

would reflect the governing principles of the Constitution—a new capital for the new nation. (*Washington Past and Present: A Guide to the Nation's Capital* (Donald R. Kennon, 1987, p. 9)

The National Mall in Washington, D.C.

The National Mall is where the past, present, and future of the United States intersect. When parents and their children visit the National Mall, they are all experiencing their first historic place-based introduction to the history of the United States. One can see how excited and interested everyone is in the memorials, government buildings, museums, and the Mall itself. This level of enthusiasm is rarely exhibited in school classrooms where students read the chapter in the text and then answer the questions at the end. What is happening at the National Mall is that we can learn with our own eyes and all of our senses that the past is part of our present and future.

These visitors are using maps, either online or as hard copies, to figure out where they are and the relationship to all that is to be seen on the Mall. The size of the National Mall with the Washington Monument and other memorials, along with the White House, Capitol, and Supreme Court, provides the visual proof of our Republic with the three branches of government. All of these places convey the message that big decisions about our country happened here and continue to happen here.

Quietly to themselves, parents start thinking of questions while the new young historians with them ask out loud: "Who were George Washington, Thomas Jefferson, Abraham Lincoln, and Dr. Martin Luther King, Jr.? What did they do? Where is Gettysburg? Can we play on the Mall and what else is this used for? Can we visit the museum about American Indians and what was the Holocaust? Why are so many people waiting in line to see the Charters of Freedom and what are they?" All of these questions come up because the entire family is curious to know more about this place. This is the place to start getting the answers about our country's past, present, and future. They can begin to be historians and ask, "Why is this all here and what does this mean for us today?" Visiting Washington, D.C., and specifically the National Mall, is a tradition for many schools and parents. This guide brings the National Mall to your classroom and home to visit each year of elementary school.

The National Mall is the first historic place to visit for all of you becoming guides for your students and is of such importance that it will be a return stop for every year in elementary school. There is so much to offer students about United States history, given all the historic buildings and memorials, museums, and archives and an unbelievable amount of information online from these repositories. Starting at and returning to the National Mall imparts a lifelong lesson that the past is part of the present and future of our nation.

I would begin the introduction of American history for elementary school students by using Google Earth to visit the Washington Monument on the National Mall. Then use the National Park Service web sites for the Washington Monument and the National Mall. The National Park Service is the managing entity for all the memorials and the Mall itself and has corresponding websites. The National Mall is the logical place to begin for each grade and for ongoing review. Your actual lessons will be based on the age of the students and what they already know.

A big picture tour would start just adjacent to the towering obelisk in the center of the Mall. This 55-story stone obelisk is a memorial to George Washington. If we look farther down the Mall, we see a white marble temple that is a memorial to Abraham Lincoln. Just adjacent to this memorial near the Tidal

Basin is the Thomas Jefferson Memorial, and close by the Martin Luther King, Jr. Memorial. The obvious question for students would be, "What did these people do that our country would want to honor them like this?" We would look to our right and see a very large white structure that I would tell them is the White House where the president lives. We then look in another direction and see a huge white structure with a dome. I would tell the students this is where Congress meets. Beyond that building is another huge white building with columns. This is the Supreme Court, where judges make decisions. This is the visual reality of our Republic, our representative democracy with three distinct branches. There are museums lining the Mall that offer documents, photographs, paintings, and a multitude of artifacts that display what was done in the past; all of these are primary sources.

It is not possible for all of us to do this type of introduction physically at the National Mall, but it can be done in the classroom or home, thanks to technology like Google Earth and YouTube. It takes minimal prompting for students to start asking questions about these people who are memorialized on the Mall and about how our government operates. Students could then become aware of more recent memorials for Franklin Delano Roosevelt and Martin Luther King, Jr. The discussion can lead to the involvement of these people in the founding of our country, the preservation of the Union, rights of citizenship, and other social issues. All of these topics connect to the Charters of Freedom preserved and displayed for all to see in the National Archives. Visitors to the National Mall wait in city-block long lines to see the Declaration of Independence, United States Constitution, and Bill of Rights. We all sense their importance to our lives as citizens of the United States.

The form of our Republic as a representative democracy is understood visually by visiting the buildings associated with our three branches of government and the Charters of Freedom. This type of presentation that looks at the present to develop a curiosity for the past is critical for meaningful instruction in United States history.

Once students have seen a historic place from the present and developed a curiosity, they then locate where that place is based in relation to the student's home or school. Now, reading written material and asking questions becomes valuable. The message to students is there are places where buildings and landscapes still exist today that tell us about our past and present. Recognizing the actual locations develops a spatial approach to learning where students can think of a place and its relationship to where they are now; the students can then organize information to this place. This type of learning is how all of us organize our lives. We have images in our mind that can take on the function of a map locating where we live, work, shop, and seek entertainment.

The spatial connection for the study of the past provides a meaningful way for us to organize information and make connections to future learning. The development of a cognitive map connects the location to the people, geography, and their decisions and actions. This relevant knowledge allows students to begin to answer the "why" questions using primary sources and expert positions. The ability to have discussions and ongoing questions is the result of this approach. Curiosity, learning, and discussions become a continuous cycle. The National Mall and the surrounding historic places and primary sources are the ultimate examples of how literacy concerning the history of our nation and our responsibility as citizens can become a reality. The knowledge about the Mall and surrounding resources can tell us why the United States is the nation it is today.

IMPORTANT: Teaching is an ongoing endeavor of deciding how much information can be introduced and then reviewed for understanding. This is an essential trait in the art of teaching; always be on guard to preserve curiosity in this process. In the early grades this is critical since students possess very short attention spans.

The guiding framework easily addresses expectations that school districts have for what students should attain as a level of knowledge. Teachers know these expectations as standards which are defined as a level of quality or attainment. In the next chapter I will introduce in detail the concept of standards and how they are used by teachers, as well as how they can help parents in guiding students in their learning about the nation's past.

In the early primary grades there is a standard indicated in most state departments of education guidelines that students be introduced to symbols and landmarks of our nation. Most have a connection to people of great significance in our history. When you finish your presentations at the National Mall, expansion to more locations that are symbols/landmarks of our nation is the logical next step. Independence Hall in Philadelphia connects to the development of two Charters of Freedom displayed at the National Archives. The intricate story of the Declaration of Independence and the United States Constitution began with the writing of these two documents by specific Founders in Independence Hall. New York City has several important landmarks including Federal Hall where the Bill of Rights was drafted. George Washington was sworn into office at this location and it is where the first Congress met before relocating to Philadelphia; Congress found its permanent location at the National Mall. While in New York, Ellis Island and the 911 Memorial are important stops. You could also include Fort McHenry as the place where our National Anthem, the Star-Spangled Banner, came to fruition. You would then return to the National Mall and talk about this flag that was the motivation for this composition. Students can discover that the original flag is preserved and located in the Smithsonian Museum of American History, also on the Mall. This would be a first introduction to the concept of primary sources and their value to all of us today as we seek to understand the past.

As this type of instruction proceeds, you can return to Independence Hall to talk about the Declaration of Independence and the Constitution and then return to the National Mall to visit the Charters of Freedom and see the documents. Now, discussions are real and students sense their importance. An excellent book to read to students in these early grades is *O, Say Can You See, America's Symbols, Landmarks and Inspiring Words* by Sheila A. Keenan (2004). The information from this book and other written/digital resources is recorded in the student's travelogue when addressing the history of the decisions and actions portion of the guiding framework. Reading to students is a necessary aspect of teaching for all grades.

For kindergarten and first grade students, the Washington Monument and perhaps one other memorial would be one lesson. The lesson at first could include the cognitive map indicating just the word "mall" and vocabulary words like "Founders," "declaration" and "liberty," and then reading to students from a book about George Washington and the person connected to the other memorial. I would not address the idea of the past or primary sources yet.

The next lesson would begin with the Washington Monument and proceed to the White House, the Capitol and Supreme Court buildings of our representative democracy with a review of the cognitive map and the word "mall" on their outline map of the United States. The vocabulary would be the words "republic," "president," "representative,' and "judge," as examples. A short review of the memorials could also be included.

Later visits to the National Mall in kindergarten and first

grade would include all of the memorials and branches of government. Then you can move on to other symbols and landmarks around the country. Second grade would visit these locations again but with a greater emphasis on the people connected to the symbols and landmarks of our nation including visits to their residences. In third grade, discussions about George Washington, Thomas Jefferson and other Founders would connect to a visit to Independence Hall in Philadelphia to begin to talk about the involvement of these men with the Charters of Freedom. All of this is done in short segments and as simply as possible for students to get the routine in place. The approach of visiting the symbols and landmarks of the United States will take the entire school year for kindergarten and first grade. It is important to use the guiding framework in sequence. When you reach the second portion of the framework, read from the appropriate colorfully illustrated book and have students write simple sentences in their travelogues.

"Traveling across the United States" via Google Earth can be a special event with students visiting historic places, rivers, mountains, and other physical features in our country. Throughout elementary school, students become aware that historic buildings and many locations are protected and interpreted by the National Park Service and are out there right now to experience in person. Also, they see that artifacts and documents are preserved by museums and archival libraries that can be visited online and in person. This constantly keeps the past in the forefront of the present with connections to the future. The students begin to understand that the past is part of their present and future.

The Washington Monument on the National Mall is the place that honors the towering impact of Washington's life work on the very foundation and construction of our country. If you go to the top, this monument to Washington is easily the focal point for the development of a cognitive map of the National Mall itself and all the historic buildings and museums. When visited in person, the Washington Monument speaks to the concept quoted in Chapter 1 where James Marston Fitch, the author of *Historic Preservation: Curatorial Management of the Built World* (1990, pp. xi-xii), spoke of the "two interconnected faces of consciousness." The event of actually visiting a historic place and connecting your knowledge to the physical place triggers this response of seeing and knowing. When one sees the height of this stone obelisk, the message is conveyed that George Washington was at the center from the very beginning of the United States, even to the extent of locating the capital of the country to this place. How could anyone not be curious to discover the places where Washington carried out his life's work?

The National Mall and all the resources nearby are key to teaching the history of our country. This location is valuable for the introduction of new material and the review of knowledge throughout a student's elementary school experience. The existing curriculum in elementary school can easily become fragmented, and without a guiding framework the ability of students and their teachers to organize information is impaired. The National Mall is the foundational location to aid this organization and reduces the abstract nature of the past by starting at the present. The reality that the Mall and its resources are in the present and can be visited today promotes curiosity and the desire to read, write, and discuss the past. New historic places can be introduced every year, based on what is being studied.

Guiding Framework and the National Mall

IMPORTANT: Your success with teaching your students and children using the guiding framework begins and continues with all that is available at the National Mall and the surrounding locations. This success is based on a level of knowledge about these resources attained by using the links to the online resources and the written resources included in Group A at the end of this guide.

I am now going to guide you on your first trip to the National Mall via Google Earth and step you through the guiding framework.[2] You will want to print out a map of the National Mall[3] and an outline map of the United States[4] with the actual states (but no text). Also, have a spiral notebook that will be your travelogue and a copy of the guiding framework.

Now is the time to actually go to the National Mall via Google Earth and use the guiding framework for yourself. You are now at the Google Earth page and have gone through the necessary procedures to use the system. I would first go to your home and see how interesting this approach can be. You can then indicate the National Mall in the location finder, but a simpler start is just to indicate that you want to go to the Washington Monument. I would visit the memorials, historic places, and museums individually before going to the Mall for the overview. There are tutorials and other aids to help you get comfortable with this 21st century approach to traveling the world and the United States specifically. Once you have a comfortable level of skill, it is time to think about arranging visits, first with an overview and then from the street perspective. The printed map of the Mall is beneficial for those who remember when there was no Internet. It is helpful for many of us to use a physical copy as an aid to get started and for actual field trips.

You indicated that you want to go to the Washington Monument in the location finder and I assume that you are now

---

[2] Google Earth: google.com/earth

[3] nps.gov/nama/planyourvisit/maps.htm

[4] eduplace.com/ss/maps/pds/us_nl.pdf

at your first historic place. The Washington Monument is always your first stop when visiting the National Mall to help everyone get oriented from a cognitive map standpoint. Also, it helps to make the point that George Washington was at the center of the beginning and establishment of our country. As our first president, he was the role model for future presidents and was well aware of this responsibility.

Now you will be using the guiding framework and indicate in your travelogue that the historic place we are visiting is the Washington Monument on the National Mall. The next step is to start the development of your cognitive map of historic places in the United States. You will now write on the outline map of our country where Washington, D.C., is located and indicate this location with the number 1. Next you will write the number 1 in the travelogue and label Washington, D.C., and National Mall. For very young students they might just write the number "1" and the word "mall" in their travelogue. On this map mark where you are with an "H" for home and indicate this on your travelogue with an "H" and your specific place. Later on you can have your students develop a map key that shows the number and location as well as other information.

In the later years of elementary school, students will develop extensive map keys on their travelogue maps. This begins the development of a cognitive map of historic places throughout the United States. A great deal of the information you give your students has a historic place to connect to this knowledge. Within the category of the cognitive map in the guiding framework is geography skills. To gain experience, sketch a little map of the area surrounding your home with a simple map key in your travelogue. Every school year students will develop their map skills. They will start with their school, then the area surrounding the school, the neighborhood, their town, the state, and finally the country. In reality we are starting at both ends of the spectrum. We start with their school and also our nation's capital. By fifth grade this will all merge as will their knowledge of our country.

Literacy is the next concept with the identification of new vocabulary related to the historic place being visited. If they are in first grade, words like "symbol," "monument," "president," "founder" and "leader" are certain choices. Students will also record information about the historic place being studied with simple sentences in the primary grades. Students will use a travelogue to record all their work. I suggest a spiral notebook or permanent binder so student work does not get lost. The one you are using for yourself becomes a master copy for planning purposes. You can accomplish this electronically but a hard copy is always valuable. Indicate vocabulary words with definitions used in a sentences in your travelogue. You will make the determination of new vocabulary words for your students that are appropriate for their grade. Students should develop the skill for themselves to add to their travelogue from their readings. Now all of this should be in your travelogue. This completes the first part of the framework with these three categories. Now you and your students are prepared to go on to the second part of the framework, the study of the history.

The Monument is about George Washington and honoring his critical role in the United States. What is some valuable information about Washington? What are some of the decisions and actions he took that established our nation and the presidency? How does this connect with the design of the Monument? Now the information is key and can be found online and in printed form. All grades benefit from being read to for information but especially the earliest grades. I mentioned the Keenan book about symbols and landmarks of our nation. It is a good idea to have this book and other written resources on hand for future efforts. The degree to which you read to students and show YouTube information is always a judgement call but always favor the development of literacy skills.

For your purposes now, go online and look up the Washington Monument, the National Mall, and the Mount Vernon sites. There is a multitude of educational resources online and the Park Service sites usually have an information and education link. YouTube resources are voluminous with the musical performances, documentaries, and travel destinations that are available to use. Review a few YouTube videos about the Washington Monument and record some key facts about Washington and how this monument is a symbol of Washington's involvement in the founding and development of the new nation.

The World Sites Guide video for the Washington Monument on YouTube provides a good overview to begin reviewing information.[5] I would purchase a few printed resources concerning the historic places on and surrounding the National Mall. This information and the idea of symbols connects to the next category in the framework concerning the past, present and future.

George Washington picked Washington, D.C., for our new capital and was the role model for the Executive Branch during his tenure in office. He was more than aware of the importance of these beginnings. The height of the obelisk and the placement of it on the Mall symbolizes that Washington was at the center of our new nation. His willingness to give up power after the Revolutionary War and again at the completion of two terms as president established the future of our representative democracy. This is a nation where the people are the government and we elect other citizens to administer the government for a period of time and before they return to being private citizens. George Washington set the standard for all the rest of those entering the

---

[5] youtube.com/watch?v=GzsCeIUXOCA

White House. This tradition was true in the past, the present, and hopefully the future.

The final concept in the guiding framework is primary sources. The Monument itself is a historic place and a primary source about events in our country during its construction and restoration after an earthquake. Online are letters from George Washington and speeches like his Farewell Address. An excellent resource for teachers/parents is George Washington's "Rules of Civility." There is likely no better lesson to discuss student behavior and connect students to George Washington's early recognition of behavior and success. There are books about this topic as well as YouTube resources. There was an excellent link to this topic but at the time of this book being finalized, the link was not available. This is a significant frustration with online sources but most links that I am indicating in this guide should be dependable. Record information concerning the last three categories of the guiding framework in your travelogue.

The tour you have taken as an introduction is an example of how the guiding framework is used with Google Earth, You Tube and printed resources. Again, the National Mall is visited every year of elementary school for the introduction of new historic places and information. It is also important for review purposes before going to a new historic place in another part of the nation and for research about any topic in the history of our country. All the museums have a Internet presence and images that can be downloaded.

Now is an opportune time to provide an overview of work that is to be accomplished over the years of elementary school. I provide a more detailed account of this foundational knowledge development in Chapter 3. This is in a narrative form in the context of all teachers using a curriculum with consistency throughout the entire school. In Chapters 4 and 5 the guiding framework, foundational knowledge, and standards will be presented together to illustrate how all of this can work together.

I will repeat the format from Chapter 1 with each category of the guiding framework indicated, but this time the narrative will concern the work to be accomplished.

Travel to Historic Places via the Internet and in Person

> **Travel to Historic Places via the Internet and in Person**

The National Mall and all the historic places nearby are your first stop every year of elementary school. For kindergarten and first grade, symbols and landmarks of the United States are the historic places to be visited. In addition to those that I have already mentioned, Arlington National Cemetery, Mount Rushmore, the Liberty Bell and even preserved natural places like Yellowstone National Park and the Grand Canyon could be included. These symbols are visited again in second grade purely to set the context for the individuals involved with these places. Now in second grade, their homes become the focus for the famous people memorialized on the Mall and elsewhere as the medium to understand their achievements and limitations. Many state standards put emphasis on this for second grade and it just makes sense now to begin to understand these individuals as human beings. This is the time to include more personalities who had different perspectives on the events of the time. People like Abigail Adams, Frederick Douglass, George Mason, Clara Barton, and Chief Joseph provide differing outlooks on our nation during their lifetimes. Some of these individuals' homes have been preserved. Others, like Chief Joseph, called home something that is more vast than a specific structure. Students in third grade will connect with human migration from around the world and the pathways they followed. Again, there are conflicting viewpoints concerning migration but there are excellent online resources. Often, certain general topics in world history are introduced in third grade when students look at human migration, and it is certainly relevant as a lead-in to native people. The prehistoric sites can include Mesa Verde National Park, Ocmulgee National Monument, Casa Grande Ruins National Monument, and Chaco Culture National Historic Park.

Native American reservations existing today and specifically those closer to where you live are places (often with historic significance) to visit online and in person. This is also the grade to begin to look at how our representative government with three separate branches functions on the national and state levels. In addition, locate the specific historic places in your state. In Chapter 6, I give more information for using local historic places to understand their reflection of our national and world history. The historic places in your state become the major focus for fourth grade with almost every state's standards committing at least one year to the history of the state. Chapter 6 will also introduce eras in United States history and this is the context for selecting historic places to visit in fourth grade.

Fifth grade focuses on putting together all the pieces of the puzzle which is the foundational history of the United States. Eras become the focus for specific historic locations with a more elevated approach to the National Mall and Independence Hall. Also include European colonization locations like Jamestown, Revolutionary War sites[6] like Saratoga, Minuteman Historic Park, Boston Freedom Trail, Valley Forge, and Civil War sites like Gettysburg. I list online and hard copy resources to assist with this process.

---

[6] blog.oup.com/2014/06/historic-places-american-revolution/

Cognitive Map and Geography Skills

> **Cognitive Map and Geography Skills**

There are several cognitive maps that students will develop during elementary school. In every school year, students will indicate historic places on an outline map of the United States. In kindergarten, students will draw a simple map of their home with a color coded map key. They can also do one of their classroom. In first grade you can encourage the development of a map of their school and some of the surrounding neighborhood. This can also be accomplished with the area surrounding their home. The map key can have a little more detail in first and second grades. Students in kindergarten and first grade should take a field trip around their school campus and visit a little of the surrounding neighborhood. A map of the larger community is the focus of third grade with increasing details and the introduction of scale. Fourth grade is the time for a more elaborate map of your state with physical features, historic places related to eras in United States history and a specific scale. All of this comes together with a map of the United States with physical features, historic places related to eras, and a detailed map key during fifth grade. Students in fifth grade also develop a map of the National Mall to reinforce the cognitive map they have been developing every school year. There are always modifications related to student abilities with the design of these maps. This might mean that students work in teams or individually with less emphasis on scale. The endeavor of map making is important for geography skills, cognitive map development and the ability to understand the impact of geography on past events.

REMINDER: Always begin with Google Earth to see your home, school, neighborhood, and more distant locations as well as historic places. Next, use YouTube, when appropriate, for information and clarification of the location seen on Google Earth. Then the readings and discussions have context and meaning to understand the past. In the later elementary grades, the impact of the past on the present and future will become more apparent.

Literacy and Travelogue

> **Literacy and Travelogue**

I spoke earlier about literacy and the importance of vocabulary development as a foundation block for literacy. The development of vocabulary is ongoing for every school year and for every subject area. Students need to become aware that word meanings can change based on context and subject matter.

As students begin reading, the acquisition of knowledge stimulates the necessity for questions. As you guide your students to historic sites, there are important words that will facilitate the study of history. The words "who, what, when, where, and why" are key. One could also include "how." These words are often used by journalists when writing a story and go back centuries to the beginnings of rhetoric and the Socratic approach.

The oldest, and still the most powerful, teaching tactic for fostering critical thinking is Socratic teaching. In Socratic teaching we focus on giving students questions, not answers.

We model an inquiring, probing mind by continually probing into the subject with questions. (For more information, see Foundation For Critical Thinking.[7])

IMPORTANT: The use of questions is the driving force for literacy development and the ability to form positions supported by evidence.

A typical question in elementary school would be, "Who was our first president?" The word "who" prompts an answer that is a necessary part of learning that needs to continue with another question: "Why was George Washington the first president of the United States?" It is obvious that the teacher needs to provide more information in an organized manner for students to answer the "why" questions. These words also apply to the study of history to understand the decisions and actions of people in the past.

For questions related to geography, the "where" word is an obvious choice. For the study of the past, the history of people and their decisions and actions, all these words that prompt questions apply. If we return to George Washington, the other words formulate these important questions: "Who was George Washington? What did George Washington do in his lifetime? When and where did George Washington live?" All these questions apply so that a student can answer, "Why was George Washington our first president of the United States?" A teacher or parent can then even ask a higher level question, given that the past is part of our present and future, "How does the presidency of George Washington impact our government and lives today?" This approach to questioning promotes a high degree of literacy for students as they study history. The connection to the past and present and future is strengthened with bringing in current events

---

[7] criticalthinking.org/pages/socratic-teaching/606

52 • **Historic Places of our Republic**

for your students to discover the connections and timelessness of human decisions and actions.

The travelogue is a straightforward endeavor that is ongoing for every year, and the specifics I mentioned in the first chapter continue. Students can begin the development of study skills with the continuing use of the travelogue for word definitions, information about historic places, and people and their geography work. Retaining all this information in one location (spiral notebook) sends a positive message for organization and review before moving to new topics. A format for the travelogue that allows for writing and mapping that won't fall apart and get lost takes some preparation and monitoring.

These early travelogues will be invaluable in later grades and when the students become adults. I confess that I have a bias concerning long-term interest since I saved some of my school work, award certificates, report cards, and class photographs. These are now over 50 years old and are a primary source not only to my childhood but to what schools were like a half-century ago.

IMPORTANT: A new element of literacy that I want to introduce next is the Pledge of Allegiance.

Pledge of Allegiance

The Pledge of Allegiance and public education have been partners for decades. It would be hard to imagine a school day not starting with the Pledge. The fact that this cornerstone of the public education experience is ignored except as a morning ritual needs to be changed. One would be hard-pressed to think of any other endeavor with so many possibilities from an instructional standpoint but so little used other than a requirement before attendance and announcements.

The Pledge is an important vehicle for students to discover United States history, geography, and civics. Usually, the words to the Pledge are memorized by students as early as kindergarten and sometimes the definitions to some of the words are discussed in later classes but, after that, not much. There is little historical curiosity as to how the Pledge got started, who the author was, and why it became part of the public education experience.

The disinterest in the Pledge by teachers as an ongoing instructional opportunity mirrors the current low priority of history/social studies in many classrooms. A continuing cycle of greater emphasis on reading, math, and science has pushed history aside in elementary school. The less than memorable social studies experience in the memory of teachers currently in the classroom and later as administrators adds to this cycle. The Pledge, however, can become a valuable component for instruction and current events in elementary school. This can change a student's viewpoint about history/social studies so that issues in American history and civics are viewed as ongoing and are not simply relegated to the past.

All of us can recite the Pledge at lightning speed, but when have we really thought about the words and their connections to civics instruction and events in American history?

"I pledge Allegiance to the flag of the United States of America and to the Republic for which it stands, one Nation under God, indivisible, with liberty and justice for all."

Each word in the Pledge is to be defined from a dictionary standpoint beginning in first grade and then reviewed in the ongoing years in school. A convenient approach is just before the morning Pledge. Students can now think about what they are saying and a discussion as to why we pledge to the flag evolves from this. The dictionary meanings for words of the Pledge should be in very simple terminology for kindergarten and first grade students. Always use simplicity and small amounts of knowledge for each lesson with ongoing review as the foundational knowledge concerning the Pledge develops. The words to the Pledge should be posted in a visible location as an aid for thinking about the meaning of the words.

As students continue their study of history through school, the words to the Pledge will gain greater meaning with their connection to United States history. In fourth and fifth grades, a discussion about why the Pledge was written and the changes over time gives a whole new perspective for students concerning our nation.

This discussion about the Pledge and the meaning of words begins with a definition of the words "pledge" and "allegiance." What does the act of pledging mean for each of us and how far do we carry allegiance to our country? Students need to know a simple dictionary meaning in the early primary grades, but by fourth grade, with a discussion about the Bill of Rights, these words should be revisited.

The "flag" is the ultimate patriotic symbol of our country and can be introduced with the history of the Star-Spangled Banner so that students see the connection of the past to the present. Students can then discover that this specific flag still exists and is on display in the Smithsonian American History Museum. This flag can be an introduction to the concept of primary sources. The words "flag of the United States of America" introduce the physical features of what is now the United States: the growth of the country from the original 13 colonies to 50 states as represented by the stars. The red and white stripes represent the original 13 colonies; the addition of new stars to the flag helps reinforce the growth of our country through purchase and warfare. Students in fourth grade connect these stars to westward expansion and the concept of Manifest Destiny.

The word "republic" is key to the study of United States history and can be used continuously. The events leading to the formation of our Republic could include the 13 colonies, the Declaration of Independence, the Articles of Confederation, the War for Independence, Shays' Rebellion and unrest, the Constitutional Convention, the writing of the Constitution, then the ratification debate, and the rationale for the Bill of Rights. The idea that history is the study of human endeavor can be illustrated by examining how important a role George Washington played in the critical years of establishing the Republic after the ratification.

"One nation" begins a discussion of immigration and how the United States is a nation of new arrivals. The words "under God" can begin many discussions on religious freedom, even to the point that saying the Pledge of Allegiance may be in conflict with one's religious beliefs. The words "under God" were added during the 1950s at the height of the Cold War with the pervasive fear of communism. The word "indivisible" is on the same level as "republic" and is a landmark connection to our Civil War. "Indivisible" can be a prompt to all the major events that have potentially divided the country right up to the present, including going to war. There are many additional connections to social unrest and national security. The final words of the Pledge speak to the ongoing struggle since the founding of our country to obtain "liberty and justice for all." These words can begin discussions about people in our country's past who have not been treated with justice or had the opportunity for liberty and the right to vote. These conversations dealing with the worst of human endeavor are dependent on the judgement of the teacher and how much information the student is really asking for.

The Pledge can be a reinforcing element to historic places and the events that happened there. Each word in the Pledge connects events with the people involved and their decisions and actions at specific historic places. An example would be the word "republic." As students recite the Pledge and get to the word republic, have them pause and discuss what they think of in relation to this word. It could be the three branches of our government at the Mall, the Charters of Freedom in the National Archives, or Independence Hall in Philadelphia. Some students might think of George Washington at the Constitutional Convention or Martin Luther King, Jr. and his "I Have a Dream" speech at the Mall. Students in fourth and fifth grades can review their foundational knowledge every day with the Pledge of Allegiance. I encourage teachers and parents to reinforce this as a natural evolution, not a memorization activity. The reason for the Pledge's existence and its own history connects to much of our nation's viewpoints on patriotism and current events.

> To encounter the history of the Pledge is to confront American history, warts and all. The words of the Pledge have inspired millions, but they have also been used to coerce and intimidate, to compel conformity, and to silence dissent. Their daily recitation in schools and legislatures across the nation tell [s] us as much about our anxieties as a nation as they do our highest ideals (*To The Flag*, Richard Ellis, 2005, p. xi).

History of Human Decisions and Actions

History of Human Decisions and Actions

The people, decisions, and actions that are studied every year in elementary school are specific to the historic places traveled to and also to your state standards. I have identified specific locations for the development of this foundational knowledge in this chapter and in Chapters 4 and 5. The locations and links are in the Resources section. The decisions and actions that took place connect in some manner to change. These changes are often in authority and the social order. Historians have studied these changes and then organized them to define an era. Now all the other social sciences come into play to understand these changes. Again, the study of the past is history and one uses all the other social sciences to understand these past actions.

Time and Context to the Past, Present, and Future

> **Time and Context to the Past, Present, and Future**

At best, the time context can only be addressed from a school year perspective for the primary grades. The start of a new week and then a new month with a short review as to what happened at school is an introduction to what becomes the past. At home, the same review with recognition of a special event or holiday is an opportunity to talk about the past, present, and future. A reference to a long time span like a decade or century is lost with this age of student and the idea that it is in the past is sufficient.

I discussed the complexity of the concept of the past in the last chapter and the very fact that students are getting older begins their personal connection to the idea of past time. I also mentioned in the last chapter the idea of time lines and sequence lines. The memorization of dates when an event happened has little value other than to confirm that the event was in the past. The development of a sequence line rather than a time line connects specific events in the past to discuss how one event in the past led to another event in the past. To understand this, one has to assess the changes that resulted from the decisions and actions taken. This approach supports the discussion of eras in United States history which are key to the work to be accomplished in grades four and five.

Primary Sources to Interpret the Past

Primary Sources to Interpret the Past

I will use the terms "primary sources" and "primary resources" in this book. These terms need some clarity to define the difference.

- Resources are assets that can be drawn upon in order to function.
- Sources are places, persons or things from which something originates.
- Primary means of chief importance or earliest of time of order or development.

When I am speaking about a specific item like the Declaration of Independence, it is a primary source. If I am speaking about accessing primary sources as assets that can be used for the study of the past, then they are resources.

The study of the past is supported and understood with the use of primary sources. This type of material is another invaluable feature of the National Mall. The Charters of Freedom, personal letters, artifacts, photographs, and paintings are available for all to see and use in the museums and archives along the Mall. They are all resources for the study of the past.

The activity of the teacher showing some items from their childhood is the most active and visible way to introduce the idea of the past. Students can use all their senses to connect with these remaining items from the past; the items are new in a manner of speaking upon our first experience, but they are from the past. These items also illustrate people and their decisions and actions in the past compared to the present.

The changes and expansion of communication over centuries, beginning with the printing press, are examples of this. The printing press allowed the communication of words and images to reach many people at one time. The telegraph increased this speed, and the invention of the telephone allowed this communication of words in a direct manner. The smartphone of today allows even faster and more specific communication, no matter your geographic location. Each item is a primary source to understand changes in human communication over time.

The next chapter explores curriculum, content standards, and practices to illustrate how this guiding framework will work for elementary school teachers in the classroom and for parents at home.

Chapter 3

Curriculum and Standards

"Life is Really Simple But We Insist on Making it Complicated"

We sometimes say this to ourselves, but this quote is credited to Confucius and I think it is appropriate when one mentions words like "curriculum" and "standards." A definition for the word curriculum is simply a "course of study/what is taught." The word curriculum is confusing to many people, even those within the field of education. I like the minimalist definition which is "what is taught." Standards are concerned with what students should know or be able to do.

Often standards are confused with curriculum. Here is a clear example of the difference between these two topics (from an Education Week blog): "If you've ever used Google maps, you know Google gives you a choice of different routes to get to your destination. The destination is the standard and the route is the curriculum."[8]

Given that I am your guide to prepare you to teach students about the history of the United States, I would like for you to think that the guiding framework and the work indicated in each

---

[8] blogs.edweek.org/edweek/engagement_and_reform/2013/08/ stadardsnot_curriculum_three_analogies.html

category are the route that I have provided for you to reach a foundational knowledge of United States history, the destination. To put this thought into traditional education language, the curriculum is the guiding framework with the work indicated in each category and the standard is a foundational knowledge of United States history. You can now see the importance of the guiding framework that I explained in Chapters 1 and 2.

The framework is the route that can be used to meet designated standards across the country. State departments of education across the United States all have specific content standards for history/social studies, and this guiding framework is adaptable to the various state standards. The guiding framework addresses the content standards required for elementary school teachers and provides the route to a foundational knowledge of United States history for your students and children. I would recommend that parents use the standards for the state they live in to align with what their child is learning in school. In Chapters 4 and 5 I will indicate examples of state standards and how this framework and the advice in this guide can provide the route to address the range of standards across the country.

This guide provides a 21st century vision to visit the past so that students can meet state standards as well as develop a foundational knowledge of American history. There are two types of standards in education today: first, content standards; second, literacy standards. Both types have become politicized since there is great concern as to what students learn about the history of our country and whether standards should be decided at a local, state, or federal level. An example of a content standard that exists in many state departments of education for social studies/American history is: "Students will become aware of the major symbols and landmarks of the United States." In this guide, content standards will be discussed for kindergarten through fifth grade but not specific literacy standards. As used in this guide, literacy is an ongoing endeavor associated with what is being taught every day.

Often in a discussion about curriculum and standards, another term that is important for instruction is "lesson plans." These are the formal plans for what will be taught during the time of instruction, typically for the day or several days. These plans reflect both the route and specific standards for the lesson. The guiding framework can be organized into lesson plans with examples of work indicated in each category and your state content standards. The Essential Elements of Instruction[9] and many other resources online and in print are useful in the development of lesson plans.

In past decades there was a curriculum (route) for elementary school social studies called "Expanding Horizons" which began with students learning about themselves, then their family, their community, their state and, by fifth grade, American history. I have adopted some of these perspectives into this guide when applicable. Many elements of this curriculum are still reflected in what state departments of education and school districts have designated as to what elementary school students should know (standards) about American history/social studies. As I mentioned earlier, these standards vary to some extent in every state. A consistent variable is the specific knowledge about the state where the school is located. There is also ongoing controversy about what standards should be learned regarding the history of our country, with more controversy in some states; this is another reason for the variations in standards. A basic reference for standards and curriculum can be accessed online at the National Council for the Social Studies.[10]

---

[9] everything2.com/title/Essential+Elements+of+Instruction
[10] socialstudies.org

REMINDER: History is one of the social sciences, along with geography, economics, anthropology, sociology, political science, and psychology. Historians use all of the social sciences to understand the past. When you teach about the past, the history, you are using the different social sciences in order to understand past human endeavor. One does not need to teach each social science in isolation; rather, they should be incorporated into the context of studying the past, the history. This is the perspective that I take with this guide.

The dilemma in the structure of a curriculum is what specifically needs to be taught and the sequence for students to gain the defined knowledge (standards). The sequence issue in history is usually done from a chronological perspective with textbooks often beginning with native people, then Columbus, and so on. This guide puts emphasis on starting from a historic place in the present and then discovering what happened there in the past. We then move to the development of a cognitive map of each historic place with ongoing development of geography skills for greater understanding of human actions at these historic places. Literacy skills allow students to read, write, and discuss information about past decisions and actions that happened at these locations and to explore their impact on our country.

The actual study is called "history" and focuses on the examination of people's decisions and actions in the past. Time and specific dates in the past only become valuable within the context of sequence. Students can discover the connection of one event that likely led to another with an emphasis on sequence. Students need to develop a sequence line with cause and effect rather that just looking at it from a date's perspective.

Integrated study

Finally, there are primary sources that encompass all of what was written, built, designed, painted, recorded, and created during the time studied. Primary sources indicate human

Curriculum and Standards • 65

endeavor in the past, and provide an understanding of human needs and desires over the decades and centuries. There are also secondary sources where the information was written after the time of the event, but primary sources were used in the development of the position or perspective of the writer. Both are important, with textbooks being an example of a secondary source. The guiding framework provides the route for students to begin to understand the impact of the past on the present; this can then portend our likely future.

This route begins at the simplest level with kindergarten children. The framework promotes the development of foundational knowledge of United States history and literacy for elevated classroom discussions in elementary school. Now students are able to ask and answer the "why" questions and develop arguments rather than just opinions. The understanding and use of this framework is key to your preparation as a guide.

At the beginning of middle school, coverage comes to the forefront. The goal becomes covering every date and event, and too often curiosity and understanding are lost to memorization. Excessive coverage is not much of an issue at the elementary school level, given that instruction in social studies/American history from kindergarten to fifth grade is often sporadic at best.

Currently, many lessons and discussions evolve from holidays like Presidents Day (which used to be celebrated separately as Lincoln and Washington's birthdays), Martin Luther King, Jr.'s birthday, Veterans Day and the Fourth of July. These are excellent opportunities for instruction, but they should be in context with the guiding framework. One could go to the appropriate historic place (begin at the National Mall) and then visit the actual celebration going on at the person's historic home. George Washington's home at Mount Vernon is an example, or you could choose another significant historic place via technology.

A staggered approach to American history curriculum begins in the fifth grade with the Colonial period, the War for Independence, and an introduction to the beginnings of the new nation. The eighth grade student will usually revisit early eras and proceed through Westward Expansion, the Civil War, and the ongoing industrialization of our nation. Finally, the junior year of high school often features a review of these earlier eras before entering the 20th century and moving up to the present. The senior year usually requires one semester of government and one semester of economics. There are variations to this sequence to the study of history in different state standards, but all are fragmented. World history is inserted into certain grades, usually sixth and seventh, and then revisited in high school. In certain states, world history is introduced in third grade or even earlier.

Eras are introduced during fourth and fifth grades to support a bigger view of United States history by the completion of fifth grade. I prefer to use the term "United States history" because the emphasis in this guide is after the designation of the colonies as the United States. However, all the eras are important to an understanding of our nation.

IMPORTANT: I am going off the route for guiding you about the study of our nation's history in elementary school and now make some suggestions for instruction in world history in elementary and middle school.

An overview of the history of the world is critical to understanding the ongoing migration of humanity, the development of agriculture, the explorers and trade routes with conflicts and conquests, the discovery of the Americas, and the founding of the United States. Human history is about change and the shifts in power and control of land and people. This overview of world history provides the perspective to understand the desire of our Founders to establish a new relationship with government, religious freedom, the opportunity for land ownership, and a life of freedom. World history gives the necessary context to understand the uniqueness of the ideals of the Charters of Freedom and the ongoing struggle to make them a reality in the United States. World history is also the foundation for understanding the humanities (music, art, literature) and the elevated possibilities of human endeavor. The flaw is that there is no continuation of study of United States history during sixth and seventh grades. Some level of connecting American history should continue during these years.

World history is often the emphasis for history instruction in sixth and seventh grades but can be introduced in a meaningful way in third and fourth grades. As students begin to learn about their local community and their state, the introduction of human culture is appropriate. Human migration around the world is an excellent connection to native people in what would become the United States of America.

REMINDER: Human migration fascinates all cultures. National Geographic is involved with the Walk the World Project[11] and has an online presence that is exciting for students. This migration around the world brings students to their part of the world community. This topic is controversial, like most issues about the past, with several different perspectives about human migration. I want teachers and students to be aware of this as they explore and discuss the subject of migration.

The native people of your own state are always a topic in state departments of education standards. This is an opportunity to introduce the different continents that are involved in this pathway around the world. The struggle for survival with human

---

[11] walkourworld2015.weebly.com

migration leads to the topics of hunters and gatherers and the development of agriculture. Farming allows humans to settle at specific locations as people establish destination points around the world. The necessity of water to sustain a culture becomes the emergence point as food and materials for shelter start a settlement.

Now geography reaches a new level of importance when communities evolve into civilizations with the introduction of agriculture and trade because of a nearby lake or river. Then the structure of societies and classes begins with eventual conflicts and enslavement. The struggle for organization evolves to the issue of government, how humans organize themselves, and the issue of who is in control. All human cultures/societies have these struggles that ultimately decide the structure of their society. These issues common to all human endeavor are the connection to your local community, your state, nation and the world. I devote Chapter 6 to the idea that "all history is local" which is most relevant for third through fifth grades.

In sixth and seventh grades, world history is usually the exclusive focus. The connections to United States history can continue with a comparison of cultural developments along the Mississippi River and the Nile River, for example. Such a comparison would address not only the culture along the Nile during the Egyptian era but also other cultures along the Nile, and would then allow for the contrast with cultures along the Mississippi before and after the creation of the United States.

Discussions like this elevate world history and provide sufficient coverage of our nation's past so that a return to United States history in eighth grade or the junior year in high school would be seamless. In both grades the previous study of other countries' history would also clarify why our Founders were looking for a new way of life. With these means, students could accomplish a more in-depth understanding of our founding and our Charters of Freedom in eighth grade with the return to the history of our country. Studies in world history promote a greater appreciation of the opportunities in the United States as well as the need to participate as citizens in our Republic to improve the future of our nation.

IMPORTANT: Curriculum is what is taught, the route. Standards are what students need to know and accomplish, the destinations along the way. Literacy is the goal with the ability to read, write, and speak about specific content areas in a knowledgeable manner in order to organize and support a position concerning the past.

Designing a Curriculum

If one is to design a curriculum, the structure of the learning process and how the brain functions to establish memory should be addressed. There is an excellent article in *Scientific American Mind* (July/August 2010), entitled "Making Connections," in which author Anthony J. Greene states:

> Current research indicates that the essence of memory is linking one thought to another. It means that memory is dispersed, forming in the regions of the brain responsible for language, vision, hearing, emotion and other functions. Learning and memory arise from changes in neurons as they connect to and communicate with other neurons. And it means that a small reminder can reactivate a network of neurons wired together in the course of registering the event, allowing you to experience that event anew. Remembering is reliving.

Teachers and parents can reactivate the neurons by beginning the next lesson with a short review of what was done in the previous lesson and how it connects to new learning. This reinforcement is supported by the travelogue that is consistently used and kept intact. The ongoing references to the guiding framework, the National Mall resources, and the words from the Pledge of Allegiance are critical to this review and continued connections.

This ongoing emphasis can seem to be repetitive, as I mentioned earlier in this guide. In the education world this is a concept called "spiraling." A spiral curriculum can be defined as a course of study in which students will see the same topics throughout their school career, with each encounter increasing in complexity and reinforcing previous learning.

I have taken this approach with the writing of this guide as I review certain fundamentals to the guiding framework and introduce new ideas. The balance of review and the introduction of new material is a critical skill in the art of teaching. The development of literacy for every student only becomes possible when each teacher at each grade level uses a defined curriculum and continues this balance of review and the introduction of new material. The collaborative nature of elementary school and the use of the guiding framework with the indicated work can develop student knowledge and literacy concerning our nation's history. More importantly, students can come to understand the rights and responsibilities of citizenship. This is my perspective as to why students need to study the history of the United States of America. The issue of success is in the consistency of this endeavor.

Curriculum and Consistent Use
Throughout the Grades

The single biggest problem in communication is the illusion that it has taken place.

~ George Bernard Shaw

Coming together is a beginning; keeping together is progress; working together is success.

~ Henry Ford

Two major challenges of human endeavor are communication and cooperation. This is true with a representative democracy as well as education. Even in a home setting, the expectations of parents and children for education are challenging. In schools, communication and cooperation are ongoing concerns given the topics of curriculum, standards, and student achievement. The perspectives vary between principal and staff, from grade level to grade level, and even at the same grade level.

The key element of these three concerns is curriculum, and one could add these words to the Henry Ford's quote: "Coming together with a defined curriculum is a beginning, keeping together with a defined curriculum is progress, and working together with a defined curriculum is success." The concerns of standards and student achievement can only be positive with this approach. This only happens when the principal and staff know the route for each grade level, what students did before they arrived in their classroom, and what they will do after they leave. Now success becomes possible. It is critical that the principal and staff have an understanding of the foundational knowledge that is to be achieved by the use of the guiding framework and the work indicated from kindergarten through fifth grade. For parents using this guide, it is equally important to see the bigger picture and what needs to be introduced and achieved for each grade.

Now is the time to present a narrative of the foundational knowledge of the United States that students are to attain by the end of fifth grade; this is based on my personal experiences in the classroom both in teaching and observing. I have also reviewed content standards for United States history from multiple state standards and incorporated specific topics consistent to this review. I addressed this work for each category of the guiding framework in Chapter 2 and now with a big picture view. I will also address this work in a more traditional curriculum format that references a specific group of state standards in Chapters 4 and 5.

There is a tendency for all of us to just review what is required of us within a grade level. This is an opportunity to gain an overview perspective of what is to be accomplished for all of elementary school. I know that some of you will view this as redundant, but as I said in Chapter 1, this guide mirrors the spiraling approach that I am advocating for instruction.

Foundational Knowledge of
U.S. History for Elementary School

The National Mall in Washington, D.C., is where this foundational knowledge begins and continues. If one were studying the history of any country, the logical place to begin is the capital of that nation. The learning opportunities throughout the National Mall justify the emphasis as a focal point of study for every year in elementary school to initiate new perspectives and review existing knowledge. The layout of the Mall with the three branches of our government, memorials, and museums that can be accessed by the public display that we live in a free society. This is the place to learn and celebrate our freedom and the fact that the citizens are the government; we elect other citizens to represent us for a period of time. Citizens can gather on the National Mall for celebration and protest in a peaceful manner as provided in the Bill of Rights.

A cursory review of capitals and governmental systems in Russia, China, and North Korea quickly tells a different story about their kind of government and the rights of citizenship. Students need to be knowledgeable about the freedoms in our country and the frightening oppression in these other countries. Visiting the National Mall for every year of elementary school via Google Earth, along with the concepts in the guiding framework, will allow this knowledge to become understood. I have provided an extensive inventory of resources both online and in more traditional book format to support this understanding of our freedom.

IMPORTANT: A major difference from traditional approaches is the use of Google Earth, YouTube, and other online resources. It is important to understand that I am not diminishing the critical importance of more traditional resources. The only difference is the sequence of presentation, always beginning in the present with historic places today and then going to the past for the necessary study. The development of the cognitive map is also critical to organizing the information students will be given so that they begin to value this knowledge they are gaining. This valuing is reinforced with the travelogue and the preservation of their travelogues during their years in elementary school. The message for students is that the ongoing review and the introduction of new information is developing their literacy about the history of the United States and their future responsibilities as citizens of our nation. The use and preservation of these travelogues serve as a primary source of their accomplishments in elementary school.

The introduction of United States history in the earliest grades usually begins with symbols and landmarks of our country. The National Mall fits well into this approach as the starting point to visit other locales that are symbols and landmarks of United States. Each year students can learn a little bit more about the people and the decisions and actions that happened at these of historic places. Kindergarten and first grade are where literacy skills begin to grow and it is important that these two grades be extensions of one another.

The approach to the past is very similar in first grade with many students needing another "coat of paint" with certain topics and skills before additional literacy development. Literacy is always about vocabulary and sentences, reading, writing, and questions. Class discussions follow with questions and the pursuit of more knowledge. Students who are advancing more quickly can be given additional challenges to further develop their curiosity with the opportunity to present their findings to the rest of the class.

Now is the time for students to develop a respect for review, rewriting, and reflection to provoke new questions that they might not have ever thought about before. Geography skills are introduced in the simplest of terms and are connected to the world students experience every day. This means the geography of their school, their home, and neighborhood and locations visited with their parents. The field trip around your school campus and your neighborhood can solidify basic skills in geography that extend to the design of their own maps of school and home. Kindergarten students could draw a map of their home and some of their neighborhood with help from Google Earth. Both grades should do field trips of their school campus and first graders should design maps of their school with directions and a map key. Again, Google Earth would be the first step. Discovering the types of work people do today and in the past easily leads to discovering the differences and similarities of life at their school and neighborhood today and in the past. Discussions about starting a business like a lemonade stand introduce the idea of a business and capitalism to then understand the businesses in your neighborhood and community.

A greater emphasis on people is logical for second grade with an expansion of information about people, their decisions, and actions connected to symbols and landmarks of our nation. Always start at the National Mall for review and reference. A visit to the homes of some of our Founders and later Founding Fathers and Mothers is relevant and important. Students can discover that one's home is the opportunity to learn about people and their way of life today and in the past. George Washington's home at Mount Vernon, Martin Luther King, Jr.'s home in Atlanta and Clara Barton's home in Maryland are a few of the many possibilities.

It is important to introduce individuals who had different and opposing viewpoints as an introduction to conflicts in our nation. As students begin to ask questions about why women, African-Americans, or Native Americans were not involved in the founding decisions of our nation and their inability to participate as citizens with voting rights, take this opportunity to begin the conversation about justice and injustice.

Another expansion for this grade is the introduction of one-room schools from the past. Discussions about how a student's school is structured and managed today can be compared in discussions about a one-room school. This is an excellent opportunity to examine life at schools in the past. This leads to what might have been the same or different given the location or size of your community. Students can discover that one-room schools still exist today and can be located online. These early school houses are also historic places that can be located through Google Earth and YouTube.

Now is the time to put more emphasis on the idea of primary sources to understand people from the past in greater depth. An introduction to what they wrote in letters and documents connects to who they were as people and the decisions and actions they took. The Star-Spangled Banner is a good example with a close look at Francis Scott Key and his words, the connection to Fort McHenry, and the Smithsonian American History Museum where the flag that was the inspiration is preserved.

The Star-Spangled Banner is an opportunity to introduce the Pledge of Allegiance in more depth for literacy development with dictionary definitions of each word. In second grade students begin to explore how the words of the Pledge connect to events in our past and present. Toward the end of second grade, students should pick a specific individual in the past who interests them so they can write a short biography about their choice. With guidance, students can be introduced to the research and organizing of information taken from a book(s) to tell a few events in the selected person's life. This could include where they lived (historic place) and traveled as well as the decisions and action they took. The student can indicate a few of their accomplishments and some of their written words.

This now becomes the opportunity to use primary resources to support their research and connect the actual words written by this person in a letter, speech or other document. A photograph or painting of their image can be accessed from one of many online resources on the National Mall. The message conveyed is that their studies are not an act of memorization but of

Curriculum and Standards • 77

understanding. Even students with short attention spans can, over several short lessons, express their literacy. At the end of second grade students will have made ongoing visits to the National Mall and developed a cognitive map in a simple way of the symbols and landmarks at the Mall and around our nation. Information about those locales and the decisions and actions of the people involved is understood in the context of the actual historic place. Second graders can connect people in the past to the present within their family, their school, and neighborhood and the kinds of work accomplished then and now. This age should design a more detailed map of their school and surrounding community. Students will recognize the practicality of this knowledge and the importance of the cognitive map they are developing about their home, school, and neighborhood.

In third grade, a review of content standards around the United States shows a greater diversity of approaches to topics in history. This age is ready to have their world expanded literally with an introduction to world geography and human migration. Tracing this migration is an appropriate introduction to the continents of the world and the basics of human settlement. These topics include hunters and gatherers, the development of agriculture, and the implications of this new way of life. Humans begin to organize themselves into societies or civilizations with the development of class structure and who is in control.

This is another opportunity to discuss conflicts and injustices. Conflicts at school can generate discussion concerning how their school is organized with levels of authority and decision-making for a just result. This leads to discussions of government and who is in control and why. Now, a return to the National Mall for a more in-depth look at our government and way of life versus that of other countries in the past and today brings a worldly perspective.

The words "Constitution" and "Declaration of

Independence" were mentioned in earlier grades, especially in conjunction with a visit to Independence Hall, but now greater understanding is possible. A visit via Google Earth to the National Archives on the Mall to view the Charters of Freedom is critical. Students can be read to or read the beginning sentences of the Declaration of Independence, the Preamble to the United States Constitution, and some of the key freedoms expressed in the Bill of Rights.

Again, beginning in the present at the National Mall and then going to the past reinforces the connection that the past is part of our present and future. Now, the introduction of current events is timely as students visit the Mall. Students can identify current news coming from the White House, the Capitol, and Supreme Court to see the functions of our government. A closer look at the people involved with the charters is the logical extension, along with the decisions and actions that took place related to the acceptance of these Charters. The role of citizens gains new relevance, enabling a comparison to the lives of citizens in countries with dictatorships.

An additional aspect of our Charters is the connection to the form of government that each state within the United States and even local jurisdictions have adopted. All government in the United States, at whatever level, is a representative government since in a republic/representative democracy the citizens are the government and we elect other citizens to represent us for the administration of the government. This can be the introduction to the idea that all history is local, whether it is human migration, the establishment of cultures, or the development of government. The history of each state is a reflection of the history of our nation and our representative democracy/Republic. Chapter 6 presents a closer examination of local resources to clarify this concept.

The focus on native people in the states where students live aligns with human migration and the introduction to world history. These topics are expanded in fourth grade but third graders should have an introduction to explorers and the colonization of what we call the United States as preparation for understanding eras in United States history. The map project for third grade is for students to develop a map of their state that indicates native people and colonization efforts by the country or countries that colonized the area. The geographic features of their state are included and connections to the features and where people settled is indicated with a map key.

Third grade is also an appropriate time for students to be introduced to the museums along the National Mall, the National Archives, Library of Congress, and the types of resources that each institution of preservation is involved with. A greater emphasis on reading, writing, and discussion is possible and necessary with this age. The introduction of the museums on the Mall brings more connections to primary sources and the topics of study. At this grade level, the understanding that the Declaration of Independence came first, followed by the United States Constitution, and then the Bill of Rights begins the discussion about sequence of events and their connection to one another. This generates curiosity about why this particular sequence was necessary and prompts students to ask more questions which requires more research. Toward the end of third grade, students produce a cumulative project on a relevant topic of their interest that addresses all the aspects of the guiding framework. The idea of a rubric can be introduced and the framework can be the structure for their project and evaluation.

The one consistency in state content standards across the country is the fourth grade's emphasis on the history of your state. The structure in most standards is a progression of the major eras, usually up to the present. This is an important time to introduce the meaning of eras in the history of our country and the specific eras themselves.

There are several important alignments to connect with eras in your state. The concept is that all history is local and that your state history is a reflection of our national history and the reflection begins with the same form of representative government as on a national level. Now is the opportunity to revisit the National Mall and make these connections. Additional information about the Declaration of Independence, United States Constitution, and the Bill of Rights builds knowledge about the Charters and their connections to the different eras. This is an important opportunity for students to organize the foundational knowledge they are developing that began with symbols and landmarks. The connection to current events related to the charters and our three branches of government continues. Chapter 6 provides more detailed examples of historic places and eras to identify historic places in their state that reflect the different eras.

The eras organize the changes in our nation beginning with the history of native people and their migration before there was any concept of our Charters or the United States of America. This ongoing migration brought explorers and invaders to all parts of the world including the Americas. This is another opportunity for discussions on justice and injustice related to this migration. These efforts brought the development of colonies and the desire to extract resources from new lands. What we think of as the United States today was colonized by different nations and students can understand that the origin point for the United States began with the British colonies.

The development of our Charters and the Revolutionary War were proceeding at the same time that other countries with land in North America were taking different approaches. The establishment of the United States and the Charters brought the inevitable expansion through purchase and conflict as the vision of Manifest Destiny saw a country that was destined to reach to the Pacific Ocean and the Gulf of Mexico. The expansion of the country brought slavery to the forefront with certain states abandoning the Union over slavery, resulting in the Civil War. The issue of slavery had to be resolved through this war and the result was the preservation of the Union.

The ongoing expansion of the United States after the war coincided with the accelerating Industrial Revolution and economic development. The railroad was a key player in this westward expansion, made possible by the Industrial Revolution. Now the opportunity to talk about capitalism and business and developing social issues with conflicts is relevant. The wealth generated by the ongoing expansion led to the concentration of financial fortunes in the hands of a very few citizens. Social issues would rise in the late 19th and early 20th centuries because of this concentration of wealth and the Progressive Movement began. This movement changed aspects of our federal government and state governments with direct democracy impacts that led to more direct citizen involvement.

The boom-and-bust cycle that happened several times in the 19th century would reach a great climax in the 20th century with the 1920s boom and the 1930s Great Depression. World wars would bookend these decades, with World War II ending with the use of nuclear weapons. The Korean War and the overarching Cold War would dominate most of the late decades of the 20th century.

Instruction in United States history is spread over a student's entire school career. The experience for students is that many facts are inevitably memorized for the test and then often forgotten. The emphasis on eras is the opportunity for students to get an overview of changes to our nation in a structured manner.

The state perspective in fourth grade provides the opportunity for students to get a bigger picture of our nation but in a compact way by looking at your state history and referencing the corresponding national era. Local material is especially pertinent for the study of state history. It is a balancing act to not introduce too much material that forces memorization, but rather to use the information to learn about eras and organize the relevant information. To accomplish this, students need to see historic places in your state that represent each of these eras via technology and connect these places to the national perspective. Any opportunities for in-person experiences always enhance their knowledge and interest.

The information that relates to eras is usually discussed in fourth grade but I have not observed clarification about eras discussed sufficiently. There are different perspectives on eras and for this guide I align with those from the Gilder Lehrman Institute of American History. Just as in the earlier grades, the guiding framework in total is used for each historic place. This is the time to really address the sequence line rather than one based on dates. The sequence line should be along a wall in the classroom or at home with each era indicated and then the specific historic place/event in your state indicated. It is an evolution throughout the school year with all the eras in place and the corresponding historic place/event written in as you travel around your state via Google Earth. Students will begin to identify possible causes that led to the next event or era. When the railroad arrived in your state or the territory that began your state, there will be definite changes that brought other events and the next era.

The map project for this grade would be for students to develop a map of their state that shows the physical features and the changes during the different eras. It is important for fourth and fifth grades to develop a sequence line for the different eras and the changes to their state and country. The map key could indicate the specific era the change represents. This reinforces the

Curriculum and Standards • 83

development of a cognitive map to connect the information discovered and written in their travelogues from their travels via Google Earth to the idea of sequence.

Students should do a cumulative project that connects a topic of their interest to a specific era with the state perspective and the national perspective. A review of the resource institutions on the National Mall is important and students are encouraged to use primary sources online from these institutions.

IMPORTANT: The guiding framework can be adapted to a rubric structure for students to address and use in fourth and fifth grades (see rubric link, p. 87). An excellent question for the end of fourth grade would be, "Why is our state the state it is today?" Students can start organizing their thoughts at this level to understand their state and prepare for answering the big question about our nation at the end of fifth grade.

Fifth grade continues the usual survey approach to United States history from native people to independence to Westward Expansion to the storm clouds of the Civil War. Always guard against presenting too much information that triggers the memorization of material rather than working with the material to understand what is happening. Now is the opportunity to solidify what has been learned from kindergarten to fourth grade with this bigger picture of eras that students were introduced to in fourth grade.

By fifth grade students are familiar with the three branches of government that surround the National Mall and have had discussions concerning representative government, as well as "and to the republic" from the Pledge. Students will read additional information about our representative government and learn in detail that George Washington, Thomas Jefferson, James Madison, and a host of others were first involved in the formation of our Republic and the controversies and conflicts that led to the writing of the three Charters of Freedom. These discussions take into account the need for, writing of, and eventual approval for each Charter. Current events focusing on news emanating from the White House, the Capitol, and Supreme Court connect the past to the present and future. Students will discover that current news often includes past decisions in its coverage. Now a new word for literacy appears, "precedent."

Students begin to understand why there are memorials to certain people on the Mall and revisit them through Google Earth. The National Mall would lead them to the National Archives where the Charters of Freedom are displayed. When students say the Pledge in class and say the word "republic," they are developing a cognitive map that will take them to the Mall, to the three buildings of our government, the memorials (including the most recent), and then to the National Archives where the Charters of Freedom are displayed.

Google Earth trips to Philadelphia and Independence Hall to discover who was involved at the signing of the Declaration of Independence align with discussions. Then follows a trip to Boston to walk the Freedom Trail so that students could see where and how the idea of independence began. Along the route, stop at Lexington and Concord, Valley Forge, and Yorktown, then return to Independence Hall for the Constitutional Convention and the writing of the Constitution, and debates for ratification which also included the promise of a Bill of Rights. A trip to Federal Hall in New York shows the site of where our first Congress under the new constitutional government met. This is where George Washington was sworn in as the first president and the Bill of Rights was drafted. The politics surrounding the failure to deal with the issue of slavery would take us back to the National Mall to visit the Lincoln and King

Memorials to begin to understand the issues of slavery and racism that are in glaring opposition to our Charters of Freedom. A Google Earth trip to Fort Sumter, Gettysburg and other Civil War battlefields aligns with a short overview of the Civil War.

The emphasis from many state standards is on the eras up to the start of the Civil War. The remaining eras to the present are also to be addressed but in less detail than the eras up to that point. Always use at least one historic place to visit with the more recent eras. As I mentioned for fourth grade, there are different perspectives on eras and for this guide I align with those from the Gilder Lehrman Institute of American History.

Just as in the earlier grades, the guiding framework in total is used for each historic place of an era. This is the time to put emphasis on a sequence line rather than one based on dates. The sequence line should be along a wall in the classroom or at home with each era indicated and then the specific historic place(s) and events indicated. It is an evolution throughout the school year with all the eras in place and the corresponding historic place/event written in as you travel around the nation via Google Earth. Students will begin to identify possible causation, leading to the next event or era. The map project for this grade would be for students to use an outline map of our country to indicate physical features and the changes during the different eras. The map key could indicate the specific era the change represents. This reinforces the development of a cognitive map to connect the information discovered and written in their travelogues from their travels via Google Earth.

A research project that connects a topic of a student's interest to a specific era from a national perspective is important. A review of the resource institutions on the National Mall is appropriate, given that students are to use the sources online from these institution in their project. Again, the guiding framework can be modified as a rubric structure for students to address and use with their project. The cumulative work for fifth grade is for students to answer, "Why is the United States the nation it is today?" Chapter 7 is the focus of this question. Students will already know this answer but probably not realize it.

In Chapters 4 and 5 I will illustrate how the guiding framework and the work listed under each category can be used to meet state standards and establish a foundational knowledge of United States history. Chapter 6 features the perspective that all history is local and is a key component for using local resources to develop the foundational knowledge I have indicated.

This chapter has looked at curriculum, standards, and other aspects necessary for students to learn and gain knowledge. I emphasize the use of a common curriculum throughout elementary school related to the study of United States history. This approach is just as important for all subject areas as the school reform movement in our country continues to bring this concept to the forefront. An excellent resource for more information concerning this is Mike Schmoker's book, *FOCUS: Elevating the Essentials to Radically Improve Student Learning*. On the first page of his first chapter, Schmoker supports the need for a common curriculum:

> As odd as it sounds, simple, well-known strategies and structures drive improvement in any organization (Pfeffer & Sutton, 2000). In education, this means that the general underperformance of schools can be directly attributed to a failure to implement three simple, well-known elements: a common curriculum, sound lessons, and authentic literacy. (Schmoker, 2011, p. 9)

Mike Schmoker's book provides clear advice on student learning and how to achieve improvement with your students. The following links provide additional perspective for those interested in research concerning what children can learn related to the study of history.

- Achieving History Standards in Elementary Schools
  ericdigests.org/1995-1/history.htm

- National History Education Clearinghouse
  teachinghistory.org/system/files/teachinghistory/_special-report_2011.pdf

- The Bradley Commission on History in Schools
  Building a History Curriculum: Guidelines for Teaching History in Schools:
  https://nau.edu/uploadedFiles/Academic/CAL/History/History-Social_Studies_Education/Building%20a%20History%20Curriculum.pdf

- Information and explanation of rubrics:
  cmu.edu/teaching/designteach/teach/rubrics.html

Chapter 4

Guiding Framework and California Content Standards for Social Studies

Kindergarten Through Second Grade

Overview

I've looked at social studies standards at state departments of education across the United States as well as the National Council of Social Studies standards. Teachers will need to reference the standards of their state department of education and specific requirements of their school district. Parents should review standards of the state where they reside for their own understanding and to see the standards and sequence of emphasis at each grade level, especially noting the fourth grade that traditionally covers state history. It is important to see how certain standards build on each other and reinforce the expectations at every grade. This is the way to align the efforts of teachers at each grade level and for parents to build continuity and recognize the longer perspective of expectations for students by the end of fifth grade.

I selected the California History-Social Studies Content Standards for grades K-5 for their clarity to function as a baseline

90 • **Historic Places of our Republic**

for this guide; these standards were also recognized by the Bradley Commission on History in Schools. This Commission recommended a greater emphasis on history in elementary school and marked a departure from the narrower focus as spelled out in the "Expanding Horizons" that I mentioned earlier. The California Standards represent an expansion of history and biography in K-3 with a greater emphasis on history in the upper elementary grades as well.

The Horizons approach is still in place but history is now in the forefront. Teachers and parents can use the California Standards as examples of the level of knowledge to be obtained through elementary school. The steps for each portion of the framework for each grade have two purposes: to illustrate the development of the foundational knowledge I have referenced several times and to meet the content standards narrative for the California Department of Education. Both of these steps illustrate how this guiding framework curriculum can provide the route to arrive at state departments of education standards for history/social studies in your state and the foundational knowledge I reiterate as your guide.

It is appropriate to review the words "standard," "concept," "framework," and "goal" so as to better communicate what I am expressing as your guide. As a reminder, "what is taught" defines curriculum—the route—to guide the teacher and student to the destinations that are the standards.

Standard:	A level of quality or attainment
Concept:	A general idea or understanding of something
Framework:	The basic structure or set of ideas
Goal:	A desired result

An example of a standard would be what I referenced earlier: Students recognize national and state symbols and landmarks;

this is indicated as a standard in kindergarten, first grade and again in third grade for California. This standard becomes a concept in that students need to know what symbols are. If we look at the past events that led to the creation of our national and state symbols, this becomes a study of the history of these symbols. We need to discover who was involved, what happened, when it occurred, where it occurred and, combining all of this information together, to answer why they are the symbols of the United States today. To do this you would use this guiding framework to reach the goal of knowledge related to the history of these symbols.

The California Standards have two distinct elements. The first portion indicates analysis skills that students need to use in their study of history. These skills are chronological and spatial thinking, research, evidence, point of view, and historical interpretation. I have included these in total in this chapter. Then there is a narrative summary of the standards (level of attainment) for each grade level preceding the actual standards for each grade. I have reproduced only the narrative summary for each grade level for the sake of simplicity and understanding of how this guiding framework is used. The California State Content Standards for Social Studies are available online.[12]

I would suggest that parents and teachers approach their specific state content standards with a bigger picture approach: first, for what is to be attained at a specific grade level, and then for all of elementary school. The important concepts that the list of standards is reaching for will become apparent. Do not be overwhelmed with a massive list of standards and the tendency to take a checklist approach to the standards and your instruction. Review several standards to see where you can combine and simplify down to one specific concept for the student to attain.

---

[12] cde.ca.gov/be/st/ss/documents/histsocscistnd.pdf

Look at Full Text Online

I have been your guide to bring you to the point of now using the guiding framework to address standards. The framework is in two groups of three: The first is addressing historic places, the development of a cognitive map and geography skills, and the essentials of literacy. The second group of three addresses the study of history and the use of the other social sciences and the concept of time as it relates to the past/present/future, and primary sources.

I know that you are thinking that we know this already, but I am purposely illustrating the need for review. When your students start to tell you they know this, you now know they are getting it. The use of this guiding framework in that sequence will then be used to address the California Standards as indicated in the summary for each grade's standards. This is done to illustrate that the guiding framework allows for maximum flexibility to address the variations in state standards around the country and is also a user-friendly approach for parents. Teachers and parents will use this framework to guide their students and children as they discover the history of the United States.

The format for each grade will consist of a narrative summary of the standards, then the guiding framework in total, with a bulleted list of actions to use the guiding framework to address the narrative summary of the standards and foundational knowledge. This chapter addresses grades kindergarten through second grade; grades three through five will be addressed in Chapter 5.

The goal for elementary school instruction in history is the foundational knowledge indicated in each category in the guiding framework. We need to guide children in a manner that maintains and expands their natural curiosity and guards against a "paper in, paper out" memorization approach that kills this curiosity. Students need to hear that they will be traveling across the United States to visit historic places and locations across the country with Google Earth. YouTube videos and written information will show how people's decisions and actions in the past impact everyone's life today and tomorrow.

IMPORTANT: Strive for balance with students being read to and their own reading of information from printed resources as well as online. None of this will be successful without ongoing literacy development with the use of the travelogue.

I look at elementary school as having two stages of development. The beginning level is kindergarten through second grade. Skills are introduced and the routine of learning and school culture are being established. From third grade on students are mostly comfortable with the structure and established routines of school. These students can take on greater academic challenges with increasing levels of literacy. Fourth and fifth grade students demonstrate a maturity in their abilities and literacy and with proper preparation in the earlier grades, display a level of enthusiasm and quality of work that can be impressive. The two stages illustrate how important continuity of instruction and review of prior learning are for student enjoyment of learning and academic success in later grades.

California Standards Analysis Skills

Chronological and Spatial Thinking

1. Students place key events and people of the historical era they are studying in a chronological sequence and within a spatial context; they interpret time lines.
2. Students correctly apply terms related to time, including past, present, future, decade, century, and generation.

3. Students explain how the present is connected to the past, identifying both similarities and differences between the two, and how some things change over time and some things stay the same.

4. Students use map and globe skills to determine the absolute locations of places and interpret information available through a map's or globe's legend, scale, and symbolic representations.

5. Students judge the significance of the relative location of a place (e.g., proximity to a harbor, on trade routes) and analyze how relative advantages or disadvantages can change over time.

Research, Evidence, and Point of View

1. Students differentiate between primary and secondary sources.

2. Students pose relevant questions about events they encounter in historical documents, eyewitness accounts, oral histories, letters, diaries, artifacts, photographs, maps, artworks, and architecture.

3. Students distinguish fact from fiction by comparing documentary sources on historical figures and events with fictionalized characters and events.

Historical Interpretation

1. Students summarize the key events of the era they are studying and explain the historical contexts of those events.

2. Students identify the human and physical characteristics of the places they are studying and explain how those features form the unique character of those places.

3. Students identify and interpret the multiple causes and effects of historical events.

4. Students conduct cost-benefit analyses of historical and current events.

Guiding Framework and California Content Standards: K - 2 • 95

> The California Standards narrative for the grade level is indicated first. I will often add some suggestions for that specific grade level, followed by a list of the work for each category to be accomplished over the school year. All of this is done to provide a level of direction to accomplish your specific state content standards for teachers, as well as a foundational knowledge for students in the classroom or at home. Standards often seem to ignore the level of maturity and short attention span of the youngest students. Always go with simplicity and periodically check that students are understanding the information being provided.

IMPORTANT: Each category in the guiding framework aligns with the next category. Given the limitations of book layout, it isn't possible to show all the work horizontally. You need to choose items from each category, but align them horizontally so that all six categories are included in your instruction.

The Six Categories of the Guiding Framework

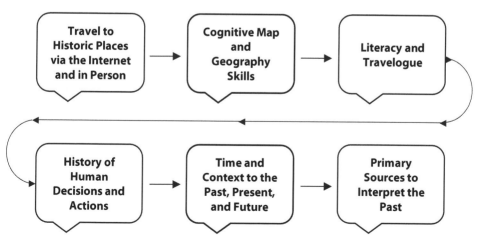

96 • **Historic Places of our Republic**

REMINDER: Don't panic! This is a school year of work for each grade and will be accomplished in short lessons several times a week.

California Standards Narrative for Kindergarten

Learning and Working Now and Long Ago

Students in kindergarten are introduced to basic spatial, temporal, and causal relationships, emphasizing the geographic and historical connections between the world today and the world long ago. The stories of ordinary and extraordinary people help describe the range and continuity of human experience and introduce the concepts of courage, self-control, justice, heroism, leadership, deliberation, and individual responsibility. Historical empathy for how people lived and worked long ago reinforces the concept of civic behavior: how we interact respectfully with each other, following rules, and respecting the rights of others.

I. Travel to Historic Places via the Internet and in Person

> **Travel to Historic Places via the Internet and in Person**

- Visit your school via Google Earth as an introduction to the possibilities.
- Visit the National Mall in Washington, D.C., via Google Earth and YouTube.
- Begin with the Washington Monument and the three buildings of our Republic.
- Future visits always start with the Washington Monument and the three buildings of our Republic. Add locations based on symbols of our country and the people involved.

Guiding Framework and California Content Standards: K - 2 • 97

- View memorials for Jefferson, Lincoln, King, Roosevelt and war memorials. Introduce Independence Hall, the Liberty Bell, the Statue of Liberty, Ellis Island, Mount Rushmore, Fort McHenry and the Star-Spangled Banner, and others of your choice.
- Use Google Earth to see physical features such as mountains, oceans, and rivers in the United States to introduce their relationship to historic places.

II. Cognitive Map and Geography Skills

> **Cognitive Map and Geography Skills**

- An outline map of the United States is a part of the student's travelogue.
- Washington, D.C., and the National Mall are labeled on the map; this is done very simply with numbers on the actual map and then the number and place written in the travelogue.
- Students at this age are just labeling the place and not each monument or memorial or detail.
- As the students travel to other locations, the new locations are done in the same manner. It may be necessary with the youngest students to help them with this process.
- Students draw on their map the locations of the Appalachian and Rocky Mountains, along with the Great Lakes, the Mississippi River, the Colorado River, the oceans and Gulf of Mexico, the Great Plains, and Southwest deserts. Use a map key with colors for different features.
- The idea of a compass and directions is put on the map and the concept of a key can be introduced.
- A class field trip around your school after seeing it on Google

Earth will introduce the use of a school map. Students review the school map and the functions that tell them how we live at school. This can introduce support discussions as to what people do at school and everyone's responsibilities.

- Students will draw a simple map of the floor plan of their own homes but not to scale; this is an introduction to design and functions that relate to how we live.

III. Literacy and Travelogue

Literacy and
Travelogue

- Each year students start a new travelogue (perhaps a spiral notebook) with outline maps.
- Students begin vocabulary lessons with words introduced from their trips to the National Mall and new locations across the country.
- As students gain information through readings and discussion, lessons in vocabulary are ongoing, with words such as "history," "past," "symbol," "leader," "memorial," "president," and "Congress" as examples to be defined and put into simple sentences.
- Words of the Pledge of Allegiance are introduced and then simply defined from a dictionary and written in the travelogue.
- Words to the Pledge are displayed for the morning recitation in the classroom for all grades to eliminate the idea that the Pledge is an endeavor of memorization.
- New vocabulary words are written in the travelogue, defined, and later used in simple sentences. This is ongoing so students will make this a habit.
- As students are read to or read on their own, they identify

other words to be defined and they will write sentences in their travelogue.

- Students use the travelogue for the entire year as a reference and for review. The message provided by retaining the travelogue is that what they wrote today is important to their learning the next day.
- The travelogue is the medium for assessment and a primary resource related to their learning over their school years. It needs to be retained as they create and add a new travelogue each year.
- Retaining the travelogue is a foundational opportunity to introduce the concept of primary sources and the past/present/future in later grades.
- Parents may want to retain the hard copy but teachers and parents should preserve a scanned copy as a record of achievement.

IMPORTANT: The introduction of landmarks and symbols of our country with Google Earth is the core to much of the work for kindergarten and first grade. The goal is to encourage the recognition that these historic places exist and can tell us much about the history of the United States; this is the beginning of geography and vocabulary skills.

REMINDER: The tour of your school is extremely important to introduce locations and beginnings of a cognitive map of their school. This is the time to begin good study habits and routines for the use of the guiding framework. All grades enjoy being read to and this is especially true for the primary grades. Their short attention spans dictate short durations for each lesson.

IV. History of Human Decisions and Actions

> **History of Human Decisions and Actions**

- People from the past are introduced as they connect to the places visited.
- The Washington Monument, memorials to Jefferson, Lincoln, and Martin Luther King, Jr. on the National Mall are connected to people and events.
- The three branches of government and what people do at each branch are introduced.
- The use of paintings and pictures and playing music illustrates human decisions and actions in the past.
- Introduce other perspectives of people's lives in the past: Abigail Adams, Harriet Tubman, Chief Joseph, among many.
- The past becomes part of the present and future as students discover how people's actions of duty and courage affect all of us today.
- The idea that the past is part of the present can be introduced simply with discussions about work their parents do and work people do at their school.
- This is an opportunity to discuss what people did for work and daily life in the past and what people do today in their work and daily life.
- Your school and neighborhood are relevant opportunities with meaningful comparisons of past and present.

V. Time and Context to the Past, Present, and Future

> **Time and Context to the Past, Present, and Future**

- The use of dates will not help students in the earliest grades.
- This is where a calendar is referenced and how hours, days, weeks, months, and finally years are recorded. This becomes a lesson in the way the past/present/future are organized.
- Later on students can begin to grasp the concept that one event often led to the next event.
- In the future you can introduce the concept that the sequence of decisions and actions and the events that happened may be planned or unplanned.
- Events through the school year can be recorded in their travelogue so that later in the year it will provide an opportunity to discuss the past/present/future at school.

VI. Primary Sources to Interpret the Past

> **Primary Sources to Interpret the Past**

This is the time for the teacher to introduce items from his/her past that inform their students about their teacher's life. You could bring a toy from childhood, a photograph of your own kindergarten class, popular music of your youth, and even school work if it was kept. The items from your own past are an excellent opportunity to convey the idea that items created during the time being studied provide a great amount of knowledge as to what life was like during that time in the past.

Students can indicate items important to their current life. This is the time to introduce music and songs of the past as well as items of daily life to reinforce what people did in the past and even today for learning and enjoyment.

REMINDER: Kindergarten is a year of introductions for these youngest students. You will see differing levels of abilities with kindergarten being an introduction to learning, and leading to a greater depth of understanding in first grade. The work I have indicated should be on the simplest of levels, and even just one or two words recorded in their travelogues is a start.

Your school and neighborhood are excellent examples to reinforce the categories of the guiding framework. This is your child or student's scope of reference and you can use each step of the framework to establish routines for learning. Use Google Earth for the introduction and then a simple map of your school or neighborhood; this can even be a sketch that you have drawn, and then your classroom or home can be marked on the map. Next would come new vocabulary to be defined, along with simple sentences about your school or neighborhood written into the travelogue. Next talk about the people, decisions, and actions that occurred. Finally, a picture or other item that shows how the school or neighborhood appeared in the past offers the opportunity to compare and contrast past and present appearances. An expansion opportunity would be to use Google Earth and YouTube to locate a one-room school and compare it to your current school. This also can be done with food markets or other locations in your neighborhood. Again, promote curiosity about the world and demonstrate the means to learn about it. Reading to students with colorfully illustrated books is very important in the primary grades.

IMPORTANT: Reading Recommendations. *O, Say Can You See, America's Symbols, Landmarks, and Inspiring Words* by Sheila Keenan and *D is for Democracy: A Citizen's Alphabet* by Elissa Grodin are excellent books to use throughout the year, adding other books for primary grades to provide more information about specific historic locations and people from the past. See Resources for additional book recommendations.

Assessment: Travelogue work and discussions.

California Standards Narrative for First Grade

A Child's Place in Time and Space

Students in grade one continue a more detailed treatment of the broad concepts of rights and responsibilities in the contemporary world. The classroom serves as a microcosm of society in which decisions are made with respect for individual responsibility, for other people, and for the rules by which we all must live: fair play, good sportsmanship, and respect for the rights and opinions of others. Students examine the geographic and economic aspects of life in their own neighborhoods and compare them to those of people long ago. Students explore the varied backgrounds of American citizens and learn about the symbols, icons, and songs that reflect our common heritage.

IMPORTANT: First grade is essentially the same work as kindergarten but the maturity of the students allows for greater understanding. The development of more vocabulary and reading ability heightens learning and discussions.

An especially important consideration for this repetition in first grade is when new students come to the school; students require this foundational work to be successful. The walking tour of the school campus can be more detailed with students designing their own school map and key from a blank template of the map of your school that is available for visitors. Students are developing a cognitive map of their school campus and attaching the information to specific locations like the library and the principal's office. They will enjoy map making and seeing the value of knowing where locations at school are and what all the adults do. This is a important endeavor for this age as they begin to value the development of a cognitive map of the historic places in our country.

I. Travel to Historic Places via the Internet and in Person

> **Travel to Historic Places via the Internet and in Person**

- Visit your school via Google Earth as an introduction to the possibilities of this technology.
- Visit the National Mall in Washington, D.C., via Google Earth and YouTube.
- Begin with Washington Monument and the three buildings of our Republic.
- Future visits always start with the Washington Monument and three buildings of our Republic. Add locations based on symbols of our country and the people involved.
- View memorials for Jefferson, Lincoln, King, Roosevelt and war memorials.
- Introduce Independence Hall, the Liberty Bell, the Statue of Liberty, Ellis Island, Mount Rushmore, Fort McHenry and the Star-Spangled Banner, Arlington Cemetery, the 911 Memorial in New York and other locations of your choice.
- Use Google Earth to show physical features such as mountains, oceans, and rivers in the United States to

introduce their relationship to historic places.

- Visit one-room schools in your region and state.

II. Cognitive Map and Geography Skills

> Cognitive Map
> and
> Geography
> Skills

- An outline map of the United States is a part of the travelogue.
- Washington, D.C., and the National Mall locations are labeled on the map; this is done very simply with numbers on the actual map and then the number and place written in the travelogue.
- Students at this age are labeling just the place and not each monument or memorial or detail.
- As the students travel to other places, the labeling is done in the same manner. It may be necessary with the youngest students to help them with this process.
- Students draw on their map where the Appalachian and Rocky Mountains are located along with the Great Lakes, the Mississippi River, the Colorado River, the Atlantic and Pacific Oceans and Gulf of Mexico, the Great Plains, and Southwest deserts. Use map key with colors for different features.
- The idea of a compass and directions are put on the map and the concept of a map key can be introduced.
- A class field trip around your school after seeing it on Google Earth will introduce the use of a school map. Students review the school map and the functions that tell them what we do at school. This can introduce support discussions about what people do at school and everyone's responsibilities. Students can draw their own map of the school using a map key with

teacher assistance. This is an opportunity for students to experience the value of maps and to understand that this is the way all of us function to find our way in the world.

- Students will draw a simple map of the floor plan of their home, label the rooms, and indicate the function. Students at this age can include more details and a map key with teacher assistance.

III. Literacy and Travelogue

Literacy and Travelogue

- Each year students start a new travelogue (perhaps a spiral notebook) with outline maps included.
- Students begin vocabulary lessons with words introduced from their trips to the National Mall and new locations across the country.
- As students gain knowledge through readings and discussions, lessons in vocabulary are ongoing with new words written in the travelogue and later used in simple sentences.
- Words to the Pledge of Allegiance are defined from a dictionary standpoint but not yet from a history point of view unless a student notices this on their own.
- Words to the Pledge are displayed for the morning recitation in the classroom for all grades so as to eliminate the idea that the Pledge is an endeavor of memorization.
- As students are read to or read on their own, they identify other words to be defined in their travelogues and write simple sentences.
- This work supports questions and answers during discussions and the possibility of new words to be defined and written in sentences.

Students use the travelogues for the entire year as a reference and for review. The message provided by retaining the travelogues is that what they wrote today is important to their ongoing learning.

- The travelogues are the medium for assessment and a primary source related to their learning over their school years and needs to be retained as they create new travelogues each year.
- Retaining the travelogues is a foundational opportunity to introduce the concept of primary resources that the students will value as they grow older.
- Parents may want to retain the hard copy but teachers and parents will want to preserve a scanned copy as a record of achievement.

IV. History of Human Decisions and Actions

> History of Human Decisions and Actions

- People from the past are introduced as they connect to the places visited.
- The Washington Monument, memorials to Jefferson, Lincoln, and Martin Luther King, Jr. on the National Mall are connected to people and events.
- The three branches of government and what people do at each branch in the past and today are discussed.
- The use of paintings and pictures and playing music illustrates human decisions and actions in the past.
- Take the opportunity to introduce other perspectives of people's lives in the past: Abigail Adams, Harriet Tubman, Chief Joseph, among many.
- The idea that the past is part of the present can be introduced

simply with discussions about work their parents do and the work people do at their school.

- This is an opportunity to discuss what people did for work and daily life in the past and what people do today in their work and daily life.
- Your school and neighborhood are relevant opportunities with meaningful comparisons of past and present.
- A one-room school from the past is an opportunity to discuss similarities and differences between today and in earlier times.
- Questions as to why women, African-Americans, and other minorities were not seen as citizens is an opportunity to discuss justice and injustice.

V. Time and Context to the Past, Present, and Future

> **Time and Context to the Past, Present, and Future**

- The use of dates will not help students in the earliest grades, so just use the term "in the past."
- This is where a calendar is referenced, along with the concept of how hours, days, weeks, months, and finally years are recorded. This is the way the past/present/future are organized. Later on students can begin to grasp the concept that one event often led to the next event.
- Students can record in their travelogues important events at their school or homes and then review a month or several months later as an example of past events.

VI. Primary Sources to Interpret the Past

> **Primary Sources to Interpret the Past**

- This is the time for the teacher to introduce items from his/her past that inform their students about their teacher's life. You can bring a toy from childhood, a photograph of your kindergarten class, popular music of your youth, and even school work if it was kept. The items from your own past are an excellent opportunity to convey the idea that items created during the time being studied provide a great amount of knowledge about what life was like in the past.
- Students can indicate items important to their life currently.
- This is the time to introduce music and songs from the past as well as daily life items to reinforce what people did in the past and do today for learning and enjoyment.
- Start introducing other items from the past in the classroom. The items can include pictures, letters and music recordings.

REMINDER: Your school and neighborhood are excellent examples to reinforce the categories of the guiding framework. This is your child or student's scope of reference and you can use each step of the framework to establish routines for learning. Use Google Earth for the introduction, then a simple map of your school or neighborhood. Introduce food markets, shopping centers, and soccer fields as opportunities to discuss your community today and in the past. Use historic photographs of your school and neighborhood as aids in discussions. Always use Google Earth; show where a location is today then show a picture of how it appeared in the past. Lead a discussion to compare changes to the neighborhood and changes to what people do today versus the past. Reading to students with colorfully illustrated books is very important in the primary grades.

IMPORTANT: Reading Recommendations. *O, Say Can You See, America's Symbols, Landmarks, and Inspiring Words* by Sheila Keenan, *The Book of Where Or How to Be Naturally Geographic* by Neill Bell, and *D is for Democracy: A Citizen's Alphabet* by Elissa Grodin. These are excellent books to use throughout the year, adding other books for primary grades that provide more information about specific historic locations and people from the past. See Resources for additional books.

Assessment: Travelogue work and discussions.

California Standards Narrative for Second Grade

People Who Make a Difference

Students in grade two explore the lives of actual people who make a difference in their everyday lives and learn the stories of extraordinary people from history whose achievements have touched them, directly or indirectly. The study of contemporary people who supply goods and services aids in understanding the complex interdependence in our free-market system.

I. Travel to Historic Places via the Internet and in Person

> **Travel to Historic Places via the Internet and in Person**

- Visit the National Mall in Washington, D.C., via Google Earth and YouTube.
- Begin with the Washington Monument and the three buildings of our Republic as a review:
  White House, Capitol, Supreme Court.
- View memorials for Jefferson, Lincoln, King, Roosevelt and the war memorials.
- Go to the homes of the people to whom the memorials are dedicated: Jefferson's Monticello, Lincoln's Springfield home, Dr. King's home in Atlanta, Washington's Mount Vernon. Go to the homes of people who were elected as president, for Congress or selected for the Supreme Court.
- Future visits: Independence Hall, Liberty Bell, Statue of Liberty, Ellis Island, Fort McHenry, Mount Rushmore, Arlington Cemetery and then the homes of people connected

112 • **Historic Places of our Republic**

to these locations. The home of Robert E. Lee is in Arlington Cemetery.

- Go to the homes or places connected to people with different stories like Chief Joseph, Harriet Tubman, Susan B. Anthony, and Frederick Douglass.
- For historic canals, bridges, pathways and trails, use Google Earth to show these locations as well as the major physical features of our country: the Mississippi River, the Great Lakes, the Rocky and Appalachian Mountains, the Atlantic and Pacific Oceans, and the Gulf of Mexico.
- Identify modes of transportation and inventions that changed our way of life and are still in use in certain areas of our country.
- Visit one-room schools, blacksmith shops, and businesses that reflect earlier ways of life in your state and the nation that are still in use today.

II. Cognitive Map and Geography Skills

> **Cognitive Map And Geography Skills**

- New outline map of U.S. with travelogue; indicate Washington, D.C., on map.
- Washington, D.C., and the National Mall locations are labeled on the map; this is done very simply with numbers on the actual map and then the number and place written in the travelogue.
- Students at this age are labeling just the place and not each monument or memorial or detail.
- Students continue their development of a cognitive map of

historic places and as best as possible label the locations of the place visited including historic homes.

- Indicate other locations on outline map of the United States when introduced: Appalachian and Rocky Mountains, the Great Lakes, the Mississippi and Colorado Rivers, the Pacific and Atlantic Oceans, the Gulf of Mexico; transportation corridors on canals, stagecoach, railroad lines, and interstate freeways. These can be drawn on the map and indicated on the map key.
- Students visit locations near school via technology and design a map of their surrounding community, including their school, with key and directions.
- The map indicates where their local government is located and perhaps their state government if they live in a capital city.
- The obvious locations include grocery stores, gas stations, and shopping centers which will connect to work and enterprise of people and family members in the community.
- The more detailed maps may work better as group projects with teams doing specific areas.

III. Literacy and Travelogue

Literacy and
Travelogue

- New travelogue using a spiral notebook or an electronic tablet. Students record all written work and map work (when possible) in travelogues.
- Pledge of Allegiance: words defined and displayed but not necessarily memorized.
- Identify new vocabulary from locations traveled to via YouTube, books, and discussions.

- Student writing and discussions become more advanced when related to the historic places and the people involved.
- This is the grade to begin to emphasize what the person was like and their qualities. Introduce the idea of biography and the importance of the written words from these people in the past.
- Connect students to the achievements and limitations of people from the past, then examine the impacts on us today.
- Students do more independent reading and writing about people from the past.
- Toward the end of the school year, students should be able to write a short biography (several sentences or more) of a person in the past who interests them and indicate why they selected this person.
- This short biography should connect to a relevant historic place and students should indicate the subject's location on a United States map as part of the finished work.
- This work should include another primary source in addition to the relevant historic place. This can be a letter or quote from a speech, for example.

IV. History of Human Decisions and Actions

History of Human Decisions and Actions

- People, decisions, and actions of key individuals from our past.
- People from the past are introduced as they connect to places visited.
- There is usually a constant relationship to the physical

geography of the place and the decisions and actions of the people involved.

- Identify the geographic features of the historic places that are visited and decide if these features are still impacts on people living today.
- Students discuss how the homes, school situation, and early lives of these people from the past impacted their later decisions and actions.
- Begin to explore what work people in your community do today and how this impacts our lives today.
- The obvious locations include grocery stores, gas stations and shopping centers.
- Introduce the idea of marketplace and how businesses function.
- Discuss how these same businesses today and in the past are similar or different.
- Discuss life in a one-room school and compare how students' lives would be different or the same as students' daily life in your school.
- Students can extend to the work their family does today and what their ancestors did in the past.
- Discuss how geography impacted their families and ancestors.

V. Time and Context to the Past, Present, and Future

> Time and Context to the Past, Present, and Future

- "Start in the present to discover the past" is a concept that needs to be introduced more actively.

116 • **Historic Places of our Republic**

- The present place always comes first and then the past of the place is introduced.
- The idea of symbols and laws that we live by today are often the same as in the past.
- All of this evolves the concept that the past is part of our present and likely future.
- Make connection to changes in transportation, inventions, and technology over time and how lives were changed.
- Begin to introduce the idea of a sequence line related to events in the past and have it posted in the classroom or a room at home. This will be the foundation work for students in future grades to see how one event led to another.

VI. Primary Sources to Interpret the Past

> Primary
> Sources to
> Interpret the
> Past

- The teacher introduces items from his/her past that inform students about their teacher's life. You can bring a toy from childhood, a photograph of your second grade class or some elementary school picture, popular music of your youth, and even school work if it was kept.
- The items from your own past are excellent devices to convey the idea that items created during the time studied provide a great amount of knowledge about what life was in the past.
- Students understand more as they see items that their teacher shares.
- Students begin to realize that their travelogues from earlier grades are a primary source for their current life in school.
- Historic places and structures are primary sources in addition

to documents, letters, recordings, and items made during the time studied.

- Students identify in their biography paper primary sources that aided in the understanding of individuals written about.
- Paintings and pictures are shown, music and songs played, and the letters of people from the past are shared.

REMINDER: Many of the locations are the same as earlier grades but now the emphasis is the connection to the people and how these people impact our lives today. This is the foundational year to address the ideas of decisions and answers along with the actual words they wrote. The spring of second grade is the time for students to work on a short biography (several sentences or more) of someone in the past who interests them. Now is also the opportunity for children to show what they are learning in an organized manner. This is expressed in writing but also from speaking about what they have learned. With the help of the teacher or parent, the student should include a primary source with the biography of the person from the past whom they selected. This could be the historic place or letter that connects to the historic person's life decisions and actions.

IMPORTANT: Recommended Readings. *O, Say Can You See, America's Symbols, Landmarks, and Inspiring Words* by Sheila Keenan, *The Book of Where Or How to Be Naturally Geographic* by Neill Bell, and *D is for Democracy: A Citizen's Alphabet* by Elissa Grodin are excellent books to use throughout the year, adding other books for primary grades that provide more information about specific historic locations and people from the past. See Resources for additional books.

Assessment: Travelogue work and discussions.

Chapter 5

Guiding Framework and California Content Standards for Social Studies

Third Through Fifth Grades

This chapter continues the use of the guiding framework to address the California Content Standards for third through fifth grades. I mentioned in Chapter 4 that I viewed elementary school in two stages, with kindergarten through second grades as the foundational years for the development of skills and routines of learning, and then an acceleration of literacy development in third through fifth grades. The format is the same as in Chapter 4, with the narrative summary of the standards and then each category of the guiding framework indicating a bulleted list of actions to address the standards and foundational knowledge. It may be helpful to review some of the introductory information in Chapter 4 concerning why I selected the California Standards and the specific analysis skills these standards endorse.

IMPORTANT: Each category in the guiding framework aligns with the next category. Given the limitations of book layout, it isn't possible to show all the work horizontally. You need to choose items from each category, but align them horizontally so that all six categories are included in your instruction.

The Six Categories of the Guiding Framework

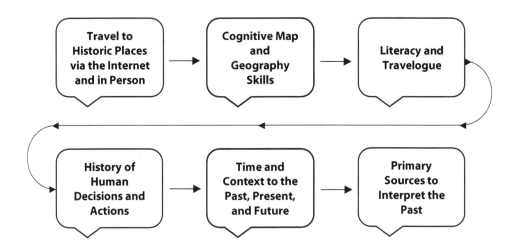

California Standards Narrative for Third Grade
Continuity and Change

Students in grade three learn more about our connections to the past and the ways in which particularly local, but also regional and national, government and traditions have developed and left their marks on current society, providing common memories. Emphasis is on the physical and cultural landscape of California, including the study of American Indians, the subsequent arrival of immigrants, and the impact they have had in forming the character of our contemporary society.

Guiding Framework and California Content Standards: 3 - 5 • 121

IMPORTANT: Third grade builds on the foundational work from the earlier grades. Some state content standards introduce world history in this grade, and the California Content Standards introduce more local and state history. It is logical to reference some context to the world given the migration of people from different continents that likely established native Americans in the Americas. The European explorers who visited North America established the various colonization efforts of the different nations at that time, including Great Britain. Given the adaptability and curiosity of humans, every state has evidence of earlier people, those who have gone before.

This is the time to introduce the development of agriculture and the start of civilizations in other parts of the world as well as in the Americas. The start of civilizations led to struggles for power and leadership. Now you can introduce government and who is in charge in the United States and your state. The context of who is in charge at your school is relevant and provides a good place to start. These same topics connect to the study of our Charters of Freedom and the rule of law.

Starting with third grade I reference some resources that are in more of a textbook format. The ten-volume series by Joy Hakim is excellent for all ages. The volume on *The First Americans* is relevant for this grade to be read to the students and then discussed. The *We The People* series of texts is written for the elementary level with an emphasis on the establishment of our government. Again, there is important material that can be read and explained to students.

I have included in this guidebook a chapter on local history which clarifies connections to local, national, and world history. Every community has local resources to reinforce and enrich third and especially fourth and fifth grades with their studies of the past.

I. Travel to Historic Places via the Internet and in Person

> **Travel to Historic Places via the Internet and in Person**

- The National Mall is always the place to start and review every year with a short look at the Washington Monument and the memorials with the perspective of connections to your region and state.
- The three branches of our Republic adjoining the Mall are visited also to make local connections and see how our representative democracy on the federal level mirrors the structure of your state as a representative democracy.
- Go to the National Archives to show where the Charters of Freedom are on display when introducing the foundation of our country's laws and ideals.
- These Charters are the basis for the structure of your local and state government. Now visit your state government buildings.
- Go to the National Mall and locate the American Indian Museum to introduce native people who live or lived in your region, state and throughout the country.
- Go to Mesa Verde National Park, Chaco Canyon National Historical Park, Casa Grande Ruins National Monument or other prehistoric and historic native people locations in your region, state and country.
- Visit Lewis and Clark National Historic Park, Lewis and Clark's Historic Trail and Nez Perce National Historical Park.
- Go to the major physical features in your state to introduce the impact of geography on human decisions and actions.

II. Cognitive Map and Geography Skills

> **Cognitive Map and Geography Skills**

- Students receive an outline map of the world and label the continents and the ocean bodies.
- Provide a new outline map of the United States with students labeling where Washington, D.C., is located and then review and label the historic landmarks/symbols they visited in the earlier grades. The locations are numbered on the map and a key indicates the place.
- Students use a map of the National Mall to mark locations of the Mall they visited in earlier grades and the new locations for this year (National Archives and American Indian Museum).
- Students indicate on an outline map of their state the state capital and their community. Students indicate and label the major physical features of their state and develop a simple map key.
- Students label prehistoric and historic places in their state.
- Students label locations and reservations of native people on their state map.
- Students design a map key of their local community at a certain scale including their school, local government location, historic places, and physical features.
- Follow the trail of Lewis and Clark and indicate interactions with native people.
- This is the time to discuss how your community began, with reference to the ability to provide food, shelter, water, and the connection to all communities in the world.
- Examine the natural resources that brought commerce and

124 • **Historic Places of our Republic**

wealth to your community initially and how the economic base may or may not have changed over time.

III. Literacy and Travelogue

> **Literacy and Travelogue**

- This year's travelogue will include all written work and outline maps for the nation, National Mall, state, and local community.
- The Pledge of Allegiance: Words are defined and students start to identify words in the Pledge that connect to events in our history.
- The words to the Pledge are displayed but students will already know it by now. The Pledge posted in large letters promotes the connection to events in the history of our country.
- Identify new vocabulary from locations traveled to, geography skills work, class discussions and readings.
- Student writing and discussions become more advanced with emphasis on connections to the historic places and the people involved.
- Students are read to and are asked to read excerpts from the Charters of Freedom and discuss.
- Current events related to the three branches of our government begin with this grade and many discussions are related to what is happening now and in the past.
- Students identify locations/places that are named based on the language of native people in their state and local community.
- Students read letters and other documents that relate to their state and community.
- Students write a short paper contrasting Native American and

Guiding Framework and California Content Standards: 3 - 5 • 125

pioneer cultures and use several primary or secondary sources based on their abilities.

IV. History of Human Decisions and Actions

> **History of Human Decisions and Actions**

- Examine people, decisions, and actions of native people, explorers and pioneers.
- Identify routes of early explorers on world map to introduce the continents of the world.
- Discuss migration of people around the world in the past and present.
- Specific peoples from the past are introduced as they connect to places visited and their actions.
- Maintain a constant focus to the physical geography of the place and the decisions and action of the people involved.
- Identify the specific geographical features of the area in which initial settlement occurred and later conflicts at these same locations, both local and state.
- Begin to identify conflicts between native people and immigrants with westward migration.
- Reference "with liberty and justice for all" in the Pledge of Allegiance and the second paragraph of the Declaration of Independence to begin discussions concerning justice and injustice.
- Encourage greater awareness and use of historical personal accounts/letters to examine decisions and actions.
- Begin to explore the involvement of government related to the conflicts between native people and new arrivals at your state and local community level.

- Identify cultural traditions and folklore at your local/state level.
- Examine the aspects of commerce that shaped the decisions of your community which impact cultural traditions and ways of life.

V. Time and Context to the Past, Present, and Future

> **Time and Context to the Past, Present, and Future**

- Start in the present to discover the past; the present place always comes first and then the past of the place is introduced.
- Introduce the concept that symbols and laws we live by today are often the same as in the past.
- Introduce and reinforce the concept that the past is part of our present and likely future.
- Students begin to see evolution of events over time and how decisions can increase or decrease conflicts.
- Students are aware of the sequence of the writing of the Charters of Freedom and begin to understand how the Declaration of Independence brought the need for the U.S. Constitution and finally the Bill of Rights.
- Use the sequence line rather than time line where the emphasis on why one event led to another event becomes more detailed. This is ongoing throughout the year and is posted for the class to see and is recorded in their travelogues.
- Begin connecting the past to the present to understand why your community is the place it is today.

VI. Primary Sources to Interpret the Past

> **Primary Sources to Interpret the Past**

- This is when the teacher introduces items from his/her past that inform the students about their teacher's life. You can bring a toy from childhood, a photograph of your kindergarten class, popular music of your youth, and even kept school work. Items from your own past are an excellent opportunity to convey the idea that items created during the time being studied provide a great amount of knowledge as to what life was like.
- Students can identify items important to their lives currently and in the recent past.
- This is the time to introduce music and songs of the past as well as items of daily life to reinforce what people did in the past and do today for learning and enjoyment.
- The travelogue is a primary source of their work in school and by third grade will begin to give the student a perspective of his/her own academic improvement with the passage of time.
- Introduce students to the field of archeology and seek out traveling trunks from local and state museums that include prehistoric artifacts like pottery sherds.
- Field trips to museums with Native American artifacts and archeological digs are appropriate for students in this grade.
- Emphasize that the historic places being visited are primary sources as are items such as paintings, pictures, music and songs that are played.

128 • **Historic Places of our Republic**

REMINDER: The maturity level of third graders and the topic of a state and local community's past set the foundation for a productive and in-depth study of your state history in fourth grade. Introductory work on the impact of human migration and explorers is clarified and expanded in fourth grade.

IMPORTANT: Recommended Readings. *Who's In Charge: How Governments Make the World Go Round*, Mary Ling, Publisher; *A History of US*, Joy Hakim; *We The People: The Citizen & The Constitution*, Center for Civic Education (Level 1); *Being an American: Exploring the Ideals that Unite Us*, The Bill of Rights Institute; *D is for Democracy: A Citizen's Alphabet*, Elissa Grodin; *The Book of Where, or How to Be Naturally Geographic*, Neill Bell. See Resources for additional recommended books.

Assessment: Travelogue work and discussions.

California Standards Narrative for Fourth Grade

California: A Changing State

Students learn the story of their home state, unique in American history in terms of its vast and varied geography, its many waves of immigration beginning with pre-Columbian societies, its continuous diversity, economic energy, and rapid growth. In addition to the specific treatment of milestones in California history, students examine the state in the context of the rest of the nation, with an emphasis on the U.S. Constitution and the relationship between state and federal government.

REMINDER: Review early explorers, trade routes, and products of trade from around the world to understand the origins of the area that you know as your state. Refer to Chapter 6 to help with this review using the local history of your community.

I. Travel to Historic Places via the Internet and in Person

> **Travel to Historic Places via the Internet and in Person**

- The National Mall is always the place to start and review every year with a short look at the Washington Monument and the memorials with the perspective of connections to your region and state.
- The three branches of our Republic are also visited to make local connections and learn how our national representative democracy mirrors the structure of your state government.
- Go to the National Archives to show where the Charters of Freedom are on display when introducing the foundation of our country's laws and ideals.
- These Charters are the basis for the structure of your local and state government. Now visit your state government buildings.
- Go to historic places in your state as they reflect eras in our history, both nationally and in your state. See Chapter 6 and Resources for advice about locating specific historic places.
- Go to the National Mall and locate the American Indian Museum, Museum of African-American History and Culture, Museum of American History and other museums located there to introduce the primary sources available to increase our understanding of people in various eras of United States history.
- Students should be introduced to the Library of Congress and the National Archives on the Mall and understand their mission and sources.
- Go to the major physical features in your state to review the

130 • Historic Places of our Republic

impact of geography on human decisions and actions that was introduced in third grade.

II. Cognitive Map and Geography Skills

> **Cognitive Map and Geography Skills**

- Provide a new outline map of the United States with students labeling where Washington, D.C., is located and then review and label the historic places they visited in earlier grades. The locations are numbered on the map and a key indicates the historic places on their map.
- Students use a map of the National Mall to mark locations on the Mall they visited in earlier grades as well as the new locations for this year: National Archives, Library of Congress, American Indian Museum, Museum of African-American History and Culture, Museum of American History and other museums that may be visited.
- Students design a map and key of their local community to a level of scale including their school, local government location, physical features, and historic places that connect to an era in United States history.
- Students design a map and key of their state to a level of scale including their community, state government location, physical features of their state, and historic places that connect to each era in their state and nation.
- Students use National Geographic "Human Journey" to identify migration patterns and the native people of their state for the era before 1620.
- Students label locations and later reservations of native people on their state maps.

III. Literacy and Travelogue

> **Literacy and Travelogue**

- This year's travelogue will include all written work and outline maps for the nation and state.
- The Pledge of Allegiance: Identify words in the Pledge that connect to events in our history and eras being studied.
- Identify new vocabulary from locations traveled to, geography skills work, class discussions, and readings.
- Student writing and discussions become more advanced and more closely related to the historic places and the people involved.
- The eras in United States history are introduced and written on the sequence line.
- Students read excerpts from the Charters of Freedom and supplemental readings that show connections to a specific era or eras.
- Current events related to the three branches of our government continue with this grade, and many discussions are possible relating to what is happening now and happened in the past.
- Students identify locations/places that are named based on the language of native people and pioneers in their state and local community.
- This is the time to discuss how your community began, with reference to the ability to secure food, shelter, and water, and discuss similarities with other locations in the nation and world.
- Examine the natural resources that enabled commerce and

132 • **Historic Places of our Republic**

wealth, and discuss how the economic base has or has not changed over time.

- Students read letters and other documents that relate to the era being studied.
- Each student selects an era in United States history that interests them to write and present a paper on how that era is reflected in the history of their state. Use the guiding framework as an outline and primary sources from local museums and archives as well as those on the National Mall.

IV. History of Human Decisions and Actions

> **History of Human Decisions and Actions**

- Discuss the people, decisions and actions of each era of our country as they are represented in your state.
- Examine the constant relationship of the physical geography of the places relevant to each era to the decisions and actions of the people involved.
- Discuss the geography of your state where initial settlements developed and discuss later conflicts at these same locations, both local and state.
- Begin to identify conflicts between native people and new arrivals as westward migration affected your state.
- Reference "with liberty and justice for all" in the Pledge of Allegiance and the second paragraph of the Declaration of Independence to begin discussions concerning justice and injustice.
- Begin to explore the involvement of government related to the conflicts between native people and new arrivals at your state and local community level.

Guiding Framework and California Content Standards: 3 - 5 • 133

- Discuss cultural traditions and folklore at your local and state levels.
- Discuss the aspects of commerce that shaped the decisions of your community and state.
- Examine the impact on cultural traditions and way of life when an era changed.

V. Time and Context to the Past, Present, and Future

> **Time and Context to the Past, Present, and Future**

- Start in the present to discover the past.
- Introduce the concept that symbols and laws that we live by today are often the same as in the past.
- Introduce and reinforce the concept that the past is part of our present and likely future.
- Students begin to see evolution of events within an era and how decisions can increase or decrease conflicts.
- Students are aware of the sequence of the writing of the Charters of Freedom and begin to understand how the Declaration of Independence brought the need for the U.S. Constitution and then the Bill of Rights.
- Develop a sequence line based on eras of your state to place emphasis on why one event led to another. This is ongoing throughout the year and is posted for the class to see and is recorded in the students' travelogues.
- Begin connecting the past to the present to understand why your state is the place it is today. These discussions will support later discussions in fifth grade as to why the United States is the nation it is today.

VI. Primary Sources to Interpret the Past

> **Primary Sources to Interpret the Past**

- The teacher introduces items from his/her past that inform students about their teacher's life.
- Bring a toy from childhood, a photograph of yourself in school, popular music of your youth, and even school work if it was kept.
- Items from your own past are an excellent opportunity to convey the idea that items created during the time being studied provide a great amount of knowledge as to what life was like at that time. Indicate any items that illustrate a specific era in our nation's past.
- Students can indicate items important both to their lives currently and to the recent past of their era.
- Historic places are primary sources with unique attributes.
- Introduce music, songs, and pictures of the eras being studied as well as items from daily life of the different eras.
- The travelogue is a primary resource of students' work in earlier grades and by fourth grade will begin to give the students a perspective of their own improvement from an academic standpoint with the passage of time.
- Encourage greater awareness and use of personal accounts, letters, and documents of a specific era.
- Review from third grade the field of archeology and seek out traveling trunks from local and state museums that include prehistoric artifacts like pottery and items of other eras.
- Schedule field trips to museums with Native American artifacts, archeological digs, and local historic sources that

illustrate different eras, such as your train station if your community has one.

REMINDER: Fourth grade is the time for students to understand how history is organized into eras. Your state history connects eras and historic places in a relatable way, given the proximity of these places. The sequence line reinforces the era concept and how one event can lead into a new era. The development of the railroad and connecting the nation by rails led to a great migration to the west. Transportation modes always align with expansion of a nation, including at the state and local levels; this is another major example of how local and national histories align. Fourth grade is an excellent time for class discussions with each student taking a specific position and then debating the issues related to an event and the resulting era. Chapter 6 and the Resources provide additional information concerning local resources and historic places related to eras.

IMPORTANT: Reading Recommendations. *Who's in Charge: How Governments Make the World Go Round*, Mary Ling; *A History of US*, Joy Hakim; *We the People: The Citizen & The Constitution*, Center for Civic Education; *Being an American: Exploring the Ideals that Unite Us*, editor Veronica Burchard; *D is for Democracy: A Citizen's Alphabet*, Elissa Grodin; and *The Book of Where, or How to be Naturally Geographic*, Neill Bell, are excellent books to use throughout the year. See the Resources section for additional book recommendations.

Assessment: Travelogues and discussions.

California Standards Narrative for Fifth Grade

U.S. History and Geography: Making a New Nation

Students in grade five study the development of the nation up to 1850, with an emphasis on the people who were already here, when and from where others arrived, and why they came. Students learn about the colonial government founded on Judeo-Christian principles, the ideals of the Enlightenment, and the English traditions of self-government. They recognize that ours is a nation that has a constitution that derives its power from the people, that has gone through a revolution, that once sanctioned slavery, that experienced conflict over land with the original inhabitants, and that experienced a westward movement that took its people across the continent. Studying the cause, course, and consequences of the early explorations through the War for Independence and western expansion is central to students' fundamental understanding of how the principles of the American republic form the basis of a pluralistic society in which individual rights are secured.

IMPORTANT: Fifth grade is where all the work of the past grades comes together as expressed in the gestalt concept I introduced earlier. All the emphasis on the categories of the guiding framework and the travelogues has given students the necessary skills for understanding the history of our nation. Typically, this grade finishes with the eras up to the Civil War. It is important for students to continue with the rest of the eras to the present. This does not mean you need to provide a tremendous amount of information for each era but just the understanding of how a few key events in one era led to the next era. It is important for students to have a sense of this progression, given that the structure of certain eras of our history is scattered throughout their entire school career. This is the opportunity for students to get a big picture of our past and become familiar with the concept of eras for United States history from their work in fourth grade. The Charters of Freedom are the other major emphasis for this grade, along with how the decisions and actions in the different eras connect to these documents. The cumulative work for students is to answer the question "Why is the United States the nation it is today?" Chapter 7 discusses the answer to this question in detail and the approach for students to understand the answer.

I. Travel to Historic Places via the Internet and in Person

> **Travel to Historic Places via the Internet and in Person**

The National Mall with the memorials and the three branches of government have been the place to start and review every year. Now the perspective of connections to the different eras in United States history is the focus. These historic places, like the Lincoln Memorial and the connection to the Civil War and the King Memorial to the later the Civil Rights movement, will now have greater meaning.

The three branches of our Republic are visited also to illuminate how our representative democracy and the decisions made connect to the eras of history in the United States.

- Go to the National Mall and show where the Charters of Freedom are on display to begin a more in-depth discussion about each document and its respective development and interpretation based on the era.

138 • **Historic Places of our Republic**

- Go to the National Mall and locate all the museums, the Library of Congress, and the National Archives as they are needed to introduce the primary sources available to enhance understanding of people in various eras of United States history.
- Travel to historic places that illustrate each era in our nation's development. See Resources for specific locations.
- Visit the key physical features in the United States as they relate to the different eras of history. An excellent illustration of this is how the routes for the railroad related to the mountain ranges and the need for the purchase or conquest of land. See Resources.

II. Cognitive Map and Geography Skills

Cognitive Map and Geography Skills

- Create new outline maps of the United States with locations of historic places that represent each era with a key and other notations. The routes of transportation modes are important to indicate on the map. When practical, more that one era can be illustrated but new maps will be needed as the eras progress.
- Students will use a map of the National Mall to highlight locations on the Mall and develop a map key that indicates an era represented for each historic place on the Mall.
- Students use National Geographic "Human Journey" to identify migration patterns of native people for the era before 1620.
- This is the time to discuss how the colonies began, with reference to the ability to provide food, shelter, water. Relate

the importance of these elements of survival and to westward expansion.

- Introduce the idea of the physical features, especially the Atlantic and Pacific Oceans as barriers to invasion from foreign countries and the Mississippi River for the transportation of supplies and people.
- Teacher/parent identifies important maps for each era to help students. See Resources.

III. Literacy and Travelogue

> **Literacy and Travelogue**

- New travelogues will include all written work, outline maps for the various eras of our nation, and the National Mall map.
- The Pledge of Allegiance: Identify words in the Pledge that connect to the eras. The era after 1945 is especially important given that words were added to the Pledge and reflect the concerns about communism in our most recent era.
- Identify new vocabulary from locations traveled to, geography skills work, class discussions and readings.
- Students writings and discussions illustrate their knowledge related to the historic places and eras being studied.
- The eras in United States history are introduced and written on a sequence time line that the entire class can see. This work should be done in groups when possible.
- Students review excerpts from the Charters of Freedom from third and fourth grades.
- Students look to the Charters to identify the relationship of these documents to the era studied and what documents were

140 • **Historic Places of our Republic**

key before and at the creation of these Charters. A short discussion about the Magna Carta is relevant.

- Discussion of current events related to the three branches of our government continues and many discussions are possible relating to what is happening now as well as in a past era.
- Examine the natural resources that enabled initial commerce and wealth and how the economic base changed with the different eras.
- Students read letters and other documents that relate to the era being studied.
- Students select an event in an era of United States history that interests them. They will select a specific event in that era to write about and present a paper using the guiding framework as an outline. Students will take a position on the event selected in the era and discuss how this led to other events of an era or following era.
- Students will answer the "big question" this year given the preparation from all the work accomplished. See Chapter 7 on "Why is the United States the nation it is today?"

IV. History of Human Decisions and Actions

> **History of Human Decisions and Actions**

- The people, decisions, and actions of each era are discussed with connections to the Charters and economic development. Changes in technology will be an ongoing part of the discussions.
- Examine the constant relationship of the physical geography of the places of each era to the decisions and actions of the people involved.

Guiding Framework and California Content Standards: 3 - 5 • 141

- Discuss the geography of our nation relevant to where initial settlements developed and move to later conflicts at these same locations.
- Begin to identify conflicts between native people and new arrivals with westward migration of the nation.
- Begin to explore the involvement of government related to the conflicts between native people and new arrivals.
- Discuss issues of human rights or lack thereof for each era. Examine who was a citizen or not, and discuss the struggles required of individuals who wished to become a citizen of our nation.
- Reference "with liberty and justice for all" in the Pledge of Allegiance and the second paragraph of the Declaration of Independence to begin discussions concerning justice and injustice.
- Discuss the aspects of commerce that shaped the decisions of our nation.
- Examine the impact on cultural traditions and way of life when an era changes.

V. Time and Context to the Past, Present, and Future

> Time and Context to the Past, Present, and Future

- Start in the present to discover the past.
- Identify the symbols and laws that we live by now and the changes from past eras.
- Introduce and reinforce the concept that the past is part of our present and likely future.
- Students begin to see the evolution of events within an era and

how decisions can increase or decrease conflicts.

- Students are aware of the sequence of the writing of the Charters of Freedom and begin to understand how the Declaration of Independence brought the need for the U.S. Constitution and then the Bill of Rights.
- The sequence line rather than a time line indicates all the eras and then specific events in our nation that correspond to the era being discussed.

VI. Primary Sources to Interpret the Past

> **Primary Sources to Interpret the Past**

- The teacher introduces items from his/her past that inform students about the teacher's life. Bring a toy from childhood, a photograph of yourself in school, popular music of your youth, and even school work if it was kept. Indicate any items that illustrate a specific era in our nation's past.
- Historic places are primary sources and connect to the eras of our nation.
- Introduce music, songs, and pictures of each era being studied as well as items from daily life of the different eras.
- The travelogue is a primary source of their work in earlier grades and by fifth grade provides the student a perspective of their own improvement from an academic and personal standpoint.
- Students will use several primary sources for their paper and access the museums on the National Mall online for images of documents, photographs, artifacts, paintings, and other primary sources for their papers.

REMINDER: Each era is examined using the guiding framework. The Resources provide all the necessary information for each category. Chapter 7 on "Why is the United States the Nation it is Today?" is important to reference along with the work in fifth grade. Students will have the skills and interest given all the previous work done in the earlier grades to accomplish the work and answer "Why is the United States the nation it is today?"

IMPORTANT: Reading Recommendations. *Who's In Charge: How Governments Make the World Go Round*, Mary Ling; *A History of US*, Joy Hakim; *We the People: The Citizen & The Constitution*, Center for Civic Education; *Being an American: Exploring the Ideals that Unite Us*, editor Veronica Burchard; *D is for Democracy: A Citizen's Alphabet*, Elissa Grodin; *The Will of the People, Readings in American Democracy*, Great Books Foundation; and *Words that Built a Nation*, Marilyn Miller, are excellent books to use throughout the year.

Assessment: Travelogue work and discussions.

Chapter 6

All History is Local

The history of a nation is made up of the history of one's family, neighborhood, town, city, and state. There are characteristics in each community that relate to communities all around the world and are part of the history of the world. This local expression of human endeavor in the past has great value for teaching history by providing examples that are in proximity to where you live. The National Mall and Washington, D.C., are the historic places to begin a study of the past, present, and future of the United States. Your state capital is the logical starting point to study the past, present and future of your state. This begins an alignment that illustrates how your state history is the local reflection of the history of our nation. The reality is that the U.S. Constitution requires that every state must have a "republican" form of government.

All history is local. It happened here–in this town. The woman's [sic] movement happened here. The Civil Rights Movement happened here–or if it did not, then the absence of African Americans or the absence of the movement is at least as important . . . These and other national and international issues affected every community, and in turn the community played a role in our national response to these issues. Viewed this way, local history is neither local nor trivial. (Loewen, 2010, p. 93)

The "Expanding Horizons" curriculum that is still part of instruction in history at the elementary school level is a reflection of this thinking. The approach begins with self and then expands to the community, state, and finally the nation. In this guide, I begin at the local level with your school and neighborhood. Students also work at the national level, locating historic places at the National Mall. There needs to be enough structure and ongoing reinforcement of the local connection in each grade for students to put this concept together as they progress with the national perspective.

I often think of a middle school social studies teacher who told me that there was no time for local history; he had to spend his class time on American history, as there were too many chapters in the text to get through before winter break. Unfortunately, this approach detached his students from many local opportunities to aid in their understanding of what they were learning in the text. This chapter provides insight to these opportunities that exist in your community and are appropriate for every grade level. The topics include family history, geography and historic places and buildings, connections to world history, cemetery research, archeology, understanding eras in the history of our country and the work of a historian.

Starting Right at Home with Our Family History

The most intimate study of the past concerns our families. This is a great opportunity for children to start comparing how life is today versus earlier times. Comparing the past to the present is common for most state standards and is an important part of the study of history. Children begin with questions about members of their family and who they were as people, where did they come from and settle? Then questions related to why they went to this place and what kind of work they did begin to evolve. Finally, there will be questions about what kinds of decisions and actions they took in their lives. These concepts are critical to the study of history. We are obviously trying to understand people and how the geography of where they lived impacted their decisions and resulting actions.

This is also an excellent opportunity for children to realize that the idea that the past is part of our present and future is a reality in their own families. The type of work your ancestors did and where they located to seek this type of work are invaluable for those living today. This knowledge helps us understand our own lives in the present and often influences our future. If there is a family business that has gone on for generations, this reality can be easily understood. Often, a similar choice of careers is part of a family's past with several generations of teachers, firefighters, or physicians. This knowledge of your family's past is accessed by photographs, letters, documents, family heirlooms and, on a larger scale, former homes and places of work. These primary sources are saved by your family, just as museums and libraries around the state and country preserve primary sources in a larger context. If these items are lost or family homes destroyed, understanding the connections to your family is greatly reduced at best.

In the process of doing history on their own family, school, or community, students will learn that their lives have larger meaning. The stories they uncover and construct will display themes that resonate across our society and over time—

immigration, working-class families having a hard time at upward mobility, the costs of war being borne by a few families. Conversely, all major events in national and world history can be seen in their impact on the local community. (Loewen, 2010, p. 95)

As an elementary school teacher, you can model exploring family history by introducing your class to your own family traditions and who you were as a child in school. This can be a great icebreaker activity to build rapport with your new students for the year with their learning more about you and the study of the past. I have often introduced a little history of my life through a suitcase activity with artifacts, documents, early recordings, and a few of my cherished toys. I have a century-old suitcase that my grandfather used with artifacts from his generation and my father's generation. I also have artifacts and things to show about my childhood and life at school. Students are always interested in my kindergarten class picture. This is an excellent approach to introducing how we study the past, and it generates curiosity for students to go home and start asking questions about their family's past. Some students might even start thinking about saving some of their own artifacts that tell their history.

This type of work connects to a local and personal perspective. It is also an introduction to primary sources and should be introduced at the same time. I'm often amused by the popularity of Facebook since people are doing many of same endeavors that historians do. These pages have photographs of what the person is doing currently with written information. Quickly, all of this becomes a part of their historical record and is really a 21st century diary.

Opportunites for In-person Experiences

As I stated in the introduction, this guide is about the importance of place in the understanding of the past. Seeing the place allows one to develop a cognitive map and arrange information and knowledge about that place in a meaningful way. Until students can actually visit places like the National Mall in person, Google Earth and YouTube allow the development of this organizational structure.

The understanding of place brings in the geography and the use of maps. Your local community abounds with opportunities for introducing the importance of maps and the local connection with the actual use of existing maps or those designed by students. I have emphasized making maps in each grade and it is important even in our digital age. An understanding of the components of a map, especially map keys and scale, is always important in daily life.

Places in your community, county, and state that have historic context give students the opportunity for an in-person experience. Children can see with their own eyes and understand what happened there. Such an experience promotes long-term retention of the history of that place. Curiosity is heightened to discover more about the buildings, landscape, and events that happened there. Children need to walk into a century-old residence and be amazed to see the past in person. A field trip to a preserved forest with houses built by the pioneers of your community is another such opportunity.

The key to success is preparation with students by first visiting this place via Google Earth and YouTube if there is a relevant video. Students will indicate where the location is on a map printed from Google Earth or other source. The map should relate to where they are now to develop their cognitive map. Now is the time to review other aspects of geography related to the historic place that is to be visited. What are the natural features still existing or have they been altered? Are the impacts from the geography involved with the significance of the place like a nearby river or other resource like timber or mineral wealth? Is this a place where different cultures have lived over hundreds of years and what were the connections to the existing physical features? This information is likely a major part of the story of this historic place.

Students then identify new vocabulary words and then formulate questions to research in the classroom and later in the field. Then discuss how this place indicates what was going on in other parts of our country, like a certain style of architecture or specific business. Now, the field trip becomes meaningful with students experiencing this historic place in person to record additional information as well as solidifying their cognitive map of this place. This process begins the understanding that their "local" history is part of their state, national, and even world history.

A Visit to World History in Your Community

Local opportunities allow students to examine the emergent location where their town or city began. There is always a water source for survival, as well as the opportunity to generate food more predictably through agriculture rather than by hunting and gathering. Finally, some regional building materials for shelter can be found, like stone, lumber, or even dirt in arid desert regions to make adobe bricks. Most often this water source, if it is on the surface, is connected with the development of transportation. Usually an identifiable natural resource that develops as an economic foundation for the community is readily apparent. This can be logging, fishing, mining, or any number of activities that often involve the extraction of resources. Then the desire grows to trade these products with other groups to obtain products not available in their region. Now comes the development of trade routes and then more efficient trade routes through exploration. This emergent locale and the available resources is a theme that relates to all cultures throughout the world. This is an important point that can connect with other communities in our state, nation and the world. The introduction of world history is now part of your local history and is an understandable approach in third grade.

Instruction in sixth and seventh grades often addresses world history but this can be introduced in a meaningful way in third and fourth grades. At these grades students also begin to learn about their local community and their state and the introduction of human culture is appropriate. Human migration around the world is an excellent connection to native people in what would become the United States of America. There are different perspectives on this migration and online resources for more information indicated in the Resources. This migration brings students to their part of the world community and to the native people who inhabited or may still live in your state today. The realization of these connections to the world with humans seeking a better way of life can be understood.

The struggle for survival leads to the topics of hunters and gatherers and the development of agriculture. Farming allowed humans to settle at specific destination points around the world. The necessity of water to sustain a culture becomes the emergence point for a settlement to begin, along with food being grown and materials located for shelter. Now geography of locations reaches a new level of importance with communities evolving into civilizations with the introduction of agriculture and trade because of a nearby lake or river. Then the structure of societies with a hierarchy of classes of people begins, followed by eventual conflict and enslavement. This struggle for organization and civilization gives rise to the issue of government and how humans organize themselves and decide who is in control. All human cultures/societies have the basic elements for survival with some structure of authority that we call "government". This is the connection to your local community, your state, nation and world.

A Visit to the Past Just Outside Your Front Door

You may reside in a very rural setting or a crowded city, but what has happened there in the past is part of the history of the United States. Elements of that history are right outside your front door, waiting to introduce American history to your students or children. You might even be within walking distance of a historic location that is of such significance that it is recognized nationally by the Department of the Interior. This recognition is designated by being listed on the National Register of Historic Places which has guidelines for qualification. This designation recognizes structures, landscapes, and locations of significant events that are worthy of recognition and preservation. The designation acknowledges certain resources and if they are destroyed, the visual and geographic resources are lost along with the essential information that only preservation can provide.

The National Park Service is part of the Department of the Interior and for the most part resources preserved and managed by the Park Service are also listed on the National Register of Historic Places. Drawings, paintings, photographs, and video are invaluable primary sources, as are historic places. The National Mall and memorials, as well as hundreds of other historic places, are under the jurisdiction of the National Park Service. There are certainly preserved areas close to where you live. All these locations have an online presence and most have extensive resources for teachers and interested parents.

The study of the past is so interconnected with the way we live our lives today. The pathways followed by native people and pioneers became the wagon trails, stagecoach routes, and railroad tracks of the 19th century and the freeways of the 20th century. The desire for communication evolved from the telegraph to the phone to the cell phone. The technology changes but the desires of human endeavor have not. Those who came before us were looking for food and shelter, a way to travel more easily, and the means by which to live together in a lawful way. Parents and teachers need to provide the message that the past is part of the present and future. These necessities of life in the past are still needed today and will be in the future. They are impacted by changes in technology but always remain. Visiting local places reinforces this message as students visit other places in the country via technology. The students need to know that this new age of technology is impacting the nation now as did the industrial age of an earlier time.

Eras in United States History

History can be organized by different perspectives such as war, economic development, entertainment, or art. Scholars have organized United States history into eras that define specific periods in the past with organizing characteristics. There are variations but I have selected those identified by the Gilder Lehrman Institute of American History[13] which has organized them by time and specific endeavors during that period. These eras are:

- Americas to 1620
- Colonization and Settlement 1585-1763
- The American Revolution 1763-1783

---

[13] gilderlehrman.org

- The New Nation 1783-1815
- National Expansion and Reform 1815-1860
- Civil War and Reconstruction 1861-1877
- Rise of Industrial America 1877-1900
- Progressive Era to New Era 1900-1929
- Great Depression and World War II 1929-1945
- 1945-to the Present

Typically in fourth grade, students learn about the history of their state by eras, but often this term and concept are not explained to students. This grade is the time that students experience a survey format with the study of history. This experience can either be an awakening to the variety of actions that humans take given the situation, or the time to start memorizing facts for the test. For students who have had sufficient preparation in an organized manner concerning the study of history in the previous grades, this can be an exciting adventure of starting to put the pieces (eras) of the past together. Putting the eras together of your state history also accomplishes this for United States history in a relatable manner.

Fourth grade students have the energy and academic skills to develop this "big picture" look at the eras in United States history. This era approach organizes the history of your state as the local reflection of our national history. Many locations in your state that are possibly only a half day or less car trip away can provide this connection to eras of your state and our nation.

A close geographic proximity opens up many places in your state to be visited by students and their teacher or parents and then to be connected to the National Mall in Washington, D.C. This connection is apparent with your state's or territory's involvement with the Civil War and the Lincoln Memorial. Lincoln will forever be connected with the end of slavery and the preservation of the Union. This same memorial will be forever connected with Dr. Martin Luther King, Jr.'s "I Have A Dream" speech and the March on Washington. The past discrimination issues in your state connect to the Civil Rights Movement and the King Memorial as well as to the Lincoln Memorial. There is a multitude of possibilities for students to connect eras of United States history to their state history. For example, if you live in Arizona, and Tucson specifically, I would guide you in this manner to connect with the different eras of our nation's past.

The earliest cultures in the Americas would be part of the era to 1620. There are many preserved and interpreted sites of this era across the United States and it is likely that your state has one. I live in the southern part of Arizona, where Casa Grande Ruins is a national monument and part of the National Park Service. This is a large prehistoric structure constructed of earthen materials by the Hohokam in 1350 C.E. and is noteworthy structure of significant size that still remains a mystery as to its original use. It is just one of many prehistoric sites that can be visited easily if you live in the Southwest. There are many historic places across the United States to discover these earliest primary resources and if it is within your state, the site is also part of your state history.

The next era dealing with colonization and settlement is represented across the United States but unless you live in what was once one of the original colonies, it is likely that the country was not England. My home in Tucson was part of Spanish colonization in what today is the southwestern portion of the United States. This is a story of conquest and conversion with missions and forts (presidios) from the explorations of Coronado onward. A portion of the presidio in Tucson has been reconstructed based on the archeological evidence at the site of the fort. There is a layering effect at many of the extraction sites with artifacts of various cultures dating back to both before and after the Spanish era. This area that I call home was under

Spanish rule while the American Revolution was ongoing.

Tucson then became part of Mexico during the era of the New Nation and National Expansion that headed west from the original colonies. This westward migration was fueled by the expansion of the railroad which infused this area with the desire of an all-weather crossing through what would later be southern Arizona. This area was still part of Mexico even after our recently-fought war with that country, the Mexican American War and the era of Manifest Destiny. The United States eventually bought additional land from Mexico in what was called the Gadsden Purchase to bring to fruition an all-weather railroad route to California. The era of the Civil War and Reconstruction would surprisingly reach to the far west with this recently purchased land being part of the Confederacy for several months before it was taken back for the Union. Arizona became its own territory before the Civil War was over, and the rise of industrial America would increase the extraction of the mineral wealth of the territory extracted.

In 1912, Arizona became the last state of the lower 48 states. Statehood occurred during the height of the Progressive Era with direct democratic laws written into the Constitution of Arizona. The Great Depression and both World Wars are represented in Tucson and throughout Arizona by buildings, military bases, and cemeteries. Tucson was once surrounded by underground missile silos during part of the Cold War in the last decades of the 20th century. One underground missile silo was preserved as a museum which contains all the launching technology, and the missile in the silo is still in place. This represents the Cold War era that began after the end of World War II in 1945.

Right Under Your Feet

A straightforward example of this connection of local places to our national history and specific eras is often right under our feet as we walk down a residential street in the older locales of our own city or town. The only stipulation is that the community that one calls home must have existed for approximately a century. There should be an impression into sidewalks that were poured in the 1930s displaying the letters "WPA" (Works Progress Administration). A field trip could be organized by teachers and parents to locate one of these impressions and then document with photography of not only the sidewalks but the houses of the neighborhood where these three letters are located. A Google Earth trip to the neighborhood and then a short PowerPoint presentation would show the sidewalk impression with the sidewalks themselves likely compromised with cracking and uplift from mature trees. Photographs would show the homes and any business storefronts from this neighborhood from an earlier time. Then you could lead a discussion as to why the sidewalk has these three-lettered impressions and what they meant would follow. The student answers should fairly quickly indicate that this impression was made by the people pouring the sidewalks. This could then lead to a discussion about who was normally in charge of accomplishing this task and the economic costs involved.

Additional research and discussion would lead to the 1930s federal government agency during the Great Depression that provided jobs for unemployed citizens through the WPA. The chain of events that led to this impression in the sidewalk could then be traced to the era of the Great Depression in the United States. More information provided by the teacher or parent would indicate that then president Franklin D. Roosevelt and his administration were dealing with the economic collapse in the country. The federal government created programs for employment and other economic supports. States with managed funds from the federal government allowed local citizens to be employed in a great diversity of work venues including the construction of roads and sidewalks. Those workers made the impressions in the sidewalk as a credit to the agency that provided the funds for the local community to employ them.

All of this research and related discussions can clarify the concept that our national history is part of our local history. These programs during the Great Depression were pervasive throughout the country, and every state and most communities that existed during this era should still have existing places exhibiting the physical results of the workers' labor.

> Old sidewalks. Often you'll find that the name of the company that put down the sidewalks is stamped into the wet cement in a few places (usually at the corner) and these stamps are often dated. Sometimes there are metal plates set into the cement. (*My Backyard History Book*, David Weitzman, 1975, p. 93)

Cemeteries are another important venue to research and discover these same connections at the local, state, and national levels. All communities have a final resting place and the older the community, the greater impact of wars and disease on the numbers of the burials.

Students can visit the older parts of a cemetery to record birth and death data on headstones. Then students can graph the number of deaths per year, and with a little research, discover the World Wars, the Korean and Vietnam Wars, and diseases such as influenza. The style and material of the gravestones, the names and wording, and the locations in the cemetery can produce more connections. Often there is a section devoted to veterans and to people of different religious beliefs. Community cemeteries are an excellent starting point to discover the history of your community. The connections continue to state, national, and even world history if an individual fought and died in a world war or epidemic.

Digging Up the Past

Archeology is defined as "the study of human activity through the recovery and analysis of material culture." The resources can include artifacts, architecture, and cultural landscapes. Students usually enjoy visiting an archeology dig in process and appreciate the opportunity to see the materials taken from the ground that are used to interpret earlier human endeavors. This can be a valuable lesson on primary sources as items are taken from the ground that can be centuries old. I have often brought ancient pottery sherds to elementary school classrooms and once they begin to understand the age and people that made them, students become interested in the opportunity to hold a fragment of a culture from a thousand years ago.

The concept of cultural layers indicated from artifacts taken out of the ground exhibits a vertical time line; this provides a different perspective from the usual horizontal time line. An archeology field trip for third grade can be meaningful and I would highly recommend such a trip with fourth graders. This experience provides students another place experience where at first glance there would be no visible connection to the past. There may be a modern building on the site but another portion of that same site with no current impacts can provide a look into the past. This always stimulates curiosity as to what may be found in all parts of their community.

An excellent example of the importance of archeology on the national level happened near Independence Hall in Philadelphia when a dig was undertaken to see if anything remained of the residence of George Washington during his presidency, before the White House existed. This made national news as enough remained to understand the floor plan of the residence and where slaves who worked at the Philadelphia White House would come and go. This visually brought to light the laws in Philadelphia at the time concerning residency and slavery. This site is now managed by the National Park Service and is an excellent opportunity to introduce archeology, cultural layers, and a horizontal sequence. This can then be expanded to the eras in the United States and how they could be visualized as a horizontal time line. This is also an excellent opportunity to discuss the conflicted and compromised views of slavery by our Founding Fathers.[14]

Buildings Have a Story to Tell

The built environment in any community displays the same impact of style and building materials in the evolution of that community's architecture and the history of a state and nation. National trends in fashion resulting from new advances in technology communicate changes in one's local history and the national story. Pioneers would use regional building materials for shelter and commerce. Advances in technology like the transcontinental railroad brought in imported construction materials and the desire for fashion. Later, the automobile transformed the nature of many cities into a very spread-out suburban style of development. Los Angeles is the classic example of the impact of the automobile and freeways in the design of a city.

Many cities have preserved earlier places in their community

[14] nps.gov/inde/learn/historyculture/history-of-the-presidents-house-site.htm

following the guidelines of the Department of the Interior for the listing on the National Register of Historic Places. There are usually online resources through local historical societies and historic preservation departments in city and state governments. There are formal inventories of places with historical significance that are preserved, thanks to the efforts of many organizations. If there are preserved places in one's own community, there are often historians who lead interpretive walking tours. I have given walking tours of historic districts and areas in Tucson, Arizona, for over thirty years. Teachers and parents can participate in a walking tour to gather information and resources to do the same for their students and children. Too often, the study of the past seems static to students, but walking tours in historic places are a perfect opportunity for students to actively explore the past and connect to the present and future.

If you're looking for a walking tour, you might want to locate what probably is the oldest part of your town. The following quote provides this perspective:

> Does your town have a Main Street, a Center Street, a First Avenue, or an "A" Street? If it does, I'll bet it's the oldest-looking street in town. And, if you look closely for the dates on the cornerstones and arches along that street, you'd find that it's lined with some of the first buildings ever built in your city. (Weitzman, 1975, p. 86)

The Work of a Historian

All the resources of one's local community can come together so that students can do the work of a historian. This is an opportunity for students to experience the detective work that historians must undertake to find answers to the "why" questions of history. Students will realize that obtaining answers that are at least close to the "truth" is difficult. This realization is very important for an understanding of current events and it is rare that the first source of information gives the entire perspective in a balanced manner.

In this process of being a detective, students need to consider the source of the information. This provokes the awareness that multiple sources are necessary to start identifying consistencies in the information from these sources. There is the element of bias to consider for written work and oral history accounts of an event. A historian needs to be skeptical and look for agendas and less than honorable motives.

The Internet connects all of us to information around the world and to many opinions disguised as fact or totally false information. The skills that students develop in the work of a historian nurtures an important mindset for the responsibilities of citizenship; these skills provide the foundation for the examination of current events. Students can discover the importance of this mindset of skepticism when "facts" are presented. This skepticism can be applied to their textbook with factual issues put into question with a detective approach in the gathering of information. This can become applicable in fourth and fifth grades. To expand on Loewen's earlier quote:

First, although students can (and should) use the web, they must not stop there. Books still exist in the library, after all. Local historical societies have archives and objects that reveal the past. People that lived through historic events remain to be interviewed. We still have the census, newspaper archives, and many other sources, many of which, unlike the web, have been vetted, making them arguably more credible. Second, every source—from the web, the library, or their textbook—needs to be annotated. The annotation—as short as a sentence or even a phrase—tells why the source is credible. Credibility is not just a matter of credentials . . . (Loewen, 2010, p. 84)

Fourth grade is the relevant time for students to begin in earnest the work of a historian. The emphasis on the history of their state and the ability to use local sources for primary research is an opportunity to be taken advantage of.

Most concisely, historiography means 'the study of history,' but not just 'studying history.' Historiography asks us to scrutinize how a given piece of history came to be. Who wrote this book? Who put up this marker? Who didn't put it up? What points of view were omitted?...Historiography is the study of why and how history changes. (Loewen, 2010, p. 68)

This is the time for students to visit a research library with archives, to put on white gloves and look at photographs, handwritten letters in envelopes with postage stamps that show that mailing a letter costs just a few cents. They can look at documents that indicate success and failures concerning the individual or event that is being researched. The facility may be old enough to have a card catalog that is still used next to the computer. Now that the student researcher has copied enough primary sources and some secondary sources like newspapers copied from microfilm, the student can start to formulate a conclusion about what they are researching to form a position about why this event or decision from the past happened. This process mandates a questioning attitude and the use of the guiding framework to organize the students' final work.

Chapter 7

The Big Question:

Why is the United States the Nation it is Today?

I posed this question several times throughout this guide and it is a key question for the basis of a foundational knowledge of United States history. This is a question that can provoke varied responses. Many adults would be overwhelmed and not know where to begin; others could begin to give a response but only after some consideration of the possibilities. Big questions promote reflection, prioritization, and organization to come up with a response. "Why" is a key word for instruction. If you substituted the definition for the word why, the question becomes, "For what reason or reasons is the United States the nation it is today?" The "why" questions are key to learning and literacy and this type of question is the foundation for classroom discussions. The National Mall and the surrounding resources are a major focus of this guide. We began our travels there and returned every year for review and new information. Then other historic places were visited, some possibly in your community or certainly in your state. These places connected to events in our nation's past, both before and after the National Mall in Washington, D.C., was established. All the events that occurred before this event brought our nation to this location and all the events after are connected in some manner to this place. This is where the question, "Why is the United States the nation it is today?" can be answered.

> Conceived in rebellion, delivered through turmoil and war, the United States of America began its existence as a conscious experiment in self-government–mankind's "last, best hope" as Abraham Lincoln would observe. Prior to 1787 the young nation was but a loose confederation; primary ties of loyalty were to local centers of power–town, county, state. Concentrated power was feared. Prevailing opinion stressed the weakness of human nature and the ease with which moral integrity and public order could be subverted. The Constitution of 1787 was designed to overcome these problems through checks and balances and the separation of powers. The Constitution was a blueprint for the new government; the planning and creation of the capital would express the same grand design. (Donald R. Kennon, 1987, p. 9)

This guide has prepared students during their years in elementary school to answer this question. Chapter 1 introduced a guiding framework that is used to understand the history of the United States.

———

Why is the United States the Nation it is Today? • 167

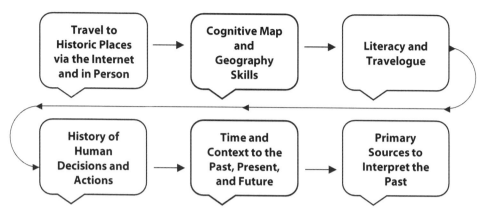

The guiding framework has been used in a sequential manner to aid in its use and success in instruction. I will use this framework to answer why the United States is the nation it is today and illustrate how all of the categories of the framework connect with each other. All the categories are necessary to put the pieces of the puzzle together to organize a position for an answer.

There are many historic places on and near the National Mall, including the monuments and memorials, the three branches of government, the National Archives, the Library of Congress, and museums. Their geographical relationship and placement contribute to answering why the United States is the nation it is today.

REMINDER: Literacy connects to the words written and spoken by those honored on the Mall. This continues with the words in the Charters of Freedom and other documents in the National Archives, the books and documents in the Library of Congress, and the artifacts and items of the Smithsonian Museums.

War defines boundaries, but it is the treaties that enforce them. Politicians win votes, but it is their speeches and laws

168 • **Historic Places of our Republic**

that effect change. And activism unites people with slogans and marches, but it is the documents that record struggle, and the proposals for change that promote civil progress. Indeed, while the actions of people defend, define, and rally for their country's success, it is their words that build a nation. (*Words that Built A Nation*, Marilyn Miller, 1999, p. 1)

The connection to these words prompts discussions concerning what the ideas expressed by these words mean. An excellent and time-tested approach is explained by the Great Books Foundation.[15] This organization endorses a "shared inquiry" format that is facilitated with "interpretative and evaluative" questions. Their publication, *Will of the People, Readings in American Democracy*, uses this shared inquiry approach to discuss the words of many of the individuals honored on the Mall and the Charters of Freedom.

IMPORTANT: As we explore, discuss, and debate the history of the United States and our role as citizens, it is necessary to include the words of Frederick Douglass, taken from Loewen's book (2009, pp. 35-36): "But it blurs an important distinction between patriotism and nationalism. Defining 'the duty of a true patriot,' Frederick Douglass wrote: 'He is a lover of his country who rebukes and does not excuse sins.' Surely teachers want to produce patriots, not nationalists." The American Heritage Dictionary defines patriotism as "love of and devotion to one's country." It defines nationalism as "devotion, especially excessive or undiscriminating to the interests or culture of a particular nation-state."

All of the following resources tell the history of decisions and actions that those from the past made and pursued. Individually,

---

[15] greatbooks.org

each is a primary source from a specific time in the past that uniquely connects us to understanding why the United States is the nation it is today.

Biographical information about each individual honored on the National Mall can be accessed by linking to the preserved homes of these people. The links are available at the end of this chapter.

Monuments and Memorials:
Touring with the Guiding Framework

Washington Monument

We start our tour on the National Mall, just as we did in Chapter 2.[16] The place to begin to learn the answer about the United States today starts with the Washington Monument.[17] I spoke earlier about the fact that the monument is in this location to symbolize that George Washington was at the center of everything related to the founding and establishment of our nation, even the selection of the site for our nation's capital. He was the general of the Revolutionary forces, presided at the Constitutional Convention and was our first president. His decision to step down from power after winning the war against England and after serving two terms as president made a nation governed by the people possible. The completion of his presidency and the first peaceful transition of power with the election of a new president has continued ever since, proving that a nation governed by the people is possible. Portions of his Farewell Address illustrate his timeless judgement for the preservation of the Republic:

---

[16] nps.gov/nama/index.htm
[17] nps.gov/wamo/index.htm

I have already intimated to you the danger of parties in the State, with particular reference to the founding of them on geographical discriminations. Let me now take a more comprehensive view, and warn you in the most solemn manner against the baneful effects of the spirit of party generally. This spirit, unfortunately, is inseparable from our nature, having its root in the strongest passions of the human mind. It exists under different shapes in all governments, more or less stifled, controlled, or repressed; but, in those of the popular form, it is seen in its greatest rankness, and is truly their worst enemy.

The alternate domination of one faction over another, sharpened by the spirit of revenge, natural to party dissension, which in different ages and countries has perpetrated the most horrid enormities, is itself a frightful despotism. But this leads at length to a more formal and permanent despotism. The disorders and miseries which result gradually incline the minds of men to seek security and repose in the absolute power of an individual; and sooner or later the chief of some prevailing faction, more able or more fortunate than his competitors, turns this disposition to the purposes of his own elevation, on the ruins of public liberty.

Without looking forward to an extremity of this kind (which nevertheless ought not to be entirely out of sight), the common and continual mischiefs of the spirit of party are sufficient to make it the interest and duty of a wise people to discourage and restrain it.

It serves always to distract the public councils and enfeeble the public administration. It agitates the community with ill-founded jealousies and false alarms, kindles the animosity of one part against another, foments occasionally riot and insurrection. It opens the door to foreign influence and corruption, which finds a facilitated access to the government itself through the channels of party passions. Thus the policy and the will of one country are subjected to the policy and will of another. (George Washington's Farewell Address, 1796)

The Washington Monument is a historic place, as are all the other monuments and memorials on the Mall. They are historic because of the focus on a specific period of time when the idea to commemorate an individual or event was deemed important as well as for the events that were happening at the time that the monument or memorial was constructed and completed. Often the actual structure and the ongoing issues in our nation at the time are symbolic. The Washington Monument was only half finished and construction stopped during our Civil War. Like our nation at that time, our country was half finished and would not be complete until the issues of slavery and preservation of the Union were resolved. The Washington Monument was completed after slavery was abolished and the Union was preserved.

The importance of developing a cognitive map of historic places is a critical part of understanding the history and development of our country. The development of the understanding of locations on the National Mall is this same idea. The Washington Monument is the tallest structure on the Mall and, from the top, one can identify the locations of the three branches of our government, the memorials, and the Mall where citizens can assemble for peaceful protests, celebrations, and recreation. The Mall geographically symbolizes our open society and liberty. It is not a coincidence that the people are at the center and the White House, Capitol and Supreme Court are at separate locations adjoining the open space of the "People's Mall."

The National Mall area we visit today is much different from the natural setting of trees and lowlands along the Potomac River in the 1790s. Roosevelt Island[18] near the Mall commemorates President Theodore Roosevelt's efforts for conservation. This area mimics the natural appearance that existed originally with forests and lowlands. There are several trails that can be explored to experience what the natural setting might have been like.

Jefferson Memorial

The Thomas Jefferson Memorial[19] celebrates this Founder's accomplishments, including his participation as the primary writer of the Declaration of Independence, the first Secretary of state, the third president of the United States and his support of the Louisiana Purchase. The words from the second paragraph of the Declaration of Independence establish life, liberty, and the pursuit of happiness:

> We hold these truths to be self-evident, that all men are created equal, that they are endowed by their Creator with certain unalienable Rights, that among these are Life, Liberty and the pursuit of Happiness. That to secure these rights, Governments are instituted among Men, deriving their just powers from the consent of the governed . . . (Declaration of Independence, 1776)

George Mason Memorial

George Mason[20] had a remarkable role in all three of the Charters of Freedom. He wrote the Virginia Declaration of Rights which

---

[18] nps.gov/this/index.htm
[19] nps.gov/thje/index.htm
[20] nps.gov/nama/planyourvisit/George-Mason-Memorial.htm

provided a framework for Jefferson to write the Declaration of Independence. Mason was a major participant at the Constitutional Convention and is famous for refusing to sign the Constitution because of slavery issues and the lack of protection for individual rights. He may be most remembered as the man responsible for the Bill of Rights.

> Regarding slavery . . . that slow poison, which is daily contaminating the minds and morals of our people. Every gentlemen here is born a petty tyrant. Practiced in acts of despotism and cruelty, we become callous to the dictates of humanity, and all the finer feelings of the soul. Taught to regard a part of our own species in the most abject and contemptible degree below us, we lose that idea of the dignity of man, which the hand of nature had implanted in us, for great and useful purposes . . . (George Mason essay, July, 1773)

Lincoln Memorial

The Lincoln Memorial[21] celebrates Abraham Lincoln's decision that slavery should be abolished and the Union preserved as the Civil War divided the nation. The warnings of George Washington in his Farewell Address about the development of parties based on geographic locations in our country and the dangers of party validate his foresight. The development of political parties aligning with geographic regions and the evil of slavery would lead to the Civil War and the dissolution of the Union. Lincoln would respond to these challenges and express his vision through the Gettysburg Address which is inscribed on one wall of the Lincoln Memorial:

---

[21] nps.gov/Linc/index.htm

174 • **Historic Places of our Republic**

Four score and seven years ago our fathers brought forth on this continent, a new nation, conceived in Liberty, and dedicated to the proposition that all men are created equal.

Now we are engaged in a great civil war, testing whether that nation, or any nation so conceived and so dedicated, can long endure. We are met on a great battle-field of that war. We have come to dedicate a portion of that field, as a final resting place for those who here gave their lives that that nation might live. It is altogether fitting and proper that we should do this.

But, in a larger sense, we can not dedicate—we can not consecrate—we can not hallow—this ground. The brave men, living and dead, who struggled here, have consecrated it, far above our poor power to add or detract. The world will little note, nor long remember what we say here, but it can never forget what they did here. It is for us the living, rather, to be dedicated here to the unfinished work which they who fought here have thus far so nobly advanced. It is rather for us to be here dedicated to the great task remaining before us -- that from these honored dead we take increased devotion to that cause for which they gave the last full measure of devotion— that we here highly resolve that these dead shall not have died in vain—that this nation, under God, shall have a new birth of freedom—and that government of the people, by the people, for the people, shall not perish from the earth. (Abraham Lincoln, November 19, 1863)

In his second inaugural address, Lincoln speaks to what the country was going through with this war and his vision for the country once the war was resolved:

Fondly do we hope—fervently do we pray—that this mighty scourge of war may speedily pass away. Yet, if God wills that it continue, until all the wealth piled by the bondsmen's two hundred and fifty years of unrequited toil shall be sunk, and until every drop of blood drawn with the lash, shall be paid by another drawn by the sword, as was said three thousand years ago, so still it must be said 'the judgments of the Lord, are true and righteous altogether.'

With malice toward none; with charity for all; with firmness in the right, as God gives us to see the right, let us strive on to finish the work we are in; to bind up the nation's wounds; to care for him who shall have borne the battle, and for his widow, and his orphan—to do all which may achieve and cherish a just, and a lasting peace, among ourselves, and with all nations. (Lincoln's Second Inaugural Address, 1865)

The Lincoln Memorial is a commemoration of Lincoln's toil for the end of slavery and the preservation of the Union. This established the memorial as the place to continue the questions of race and segregation and liberty for all the people. Celebrated American singer Marian Anderson performed there in 1937 after the Daughters of the American Revolution opposed her singing at Constitution Hall. Dr. Martin Luther King, Jr. gave his "I Have a Dream Speech" during the March on Washington at the Memorial. This March gathered at the National Mall in peaceful assembly to address grievances. The Mall is a historic place, a place for the gathering of people for significant events of protest and celebration. The people are the government and at the center in a free society. The right of peaceful assembly at the National Mall and throughout our country connects to the First Amendment of the Bill of Rights:

Congress shall make no law respecting an establishment of religion, or prohibiting the free exercise thereof; or abridging the freedom of speech, or of the press, or the right of the

176 • **Historic Places of our Republic**

people peaceably to assemble, and to petition the Government for a redress of grievances. (Bill of Rights, 1789)

Martin Luther King, Jr. Memorial

The Martin Luther King, Jr. Memorial[22] commemorates Dr. King's leadership in the long crusade for civil rights. His use of peaceful protest to unite people of all races brought change and tolerance to the nation as well as the Civil Rights Voting Act of 1965 to end racial discrimination in voting. His "I Have a Dream Speech" should be seen on YouTube and heard by every citizen of the United States. Dr. King wrote many eloquent and insightful works that were a call to action concerning the injustices in our society:

Moreover, I am cognizant of the interrelatedness of all communities and states. I cannot sit idly by in Atlanta and not be concerned about what happens in Birmingham. Injustice anywhere is a threat to justice everywhere. We are caught in an inescapable network of mutuality, tied in a single garment of destiny. Whatever affects one directly affects all indirectly. Never again can we afford to live with the narrow, provincial "outside agitator" idea. Anyone who lives inside the United States can never be considered an outsider. (Dr. Martin Luther King, Jr., Letter From the Birmingham Jail, 1963)

I have a dream that one day this nation will rise up and live out the true meaning of its creed: 'We hold these truths to be self-evident, that all men are created equal.'

I have a dream that one day on the red hills of Georgia, the sons of former slaves and the sons of former slave owners

---

[22] nps.gov/mlkm/index.htm

will be able to sit down together at the table of brotherhood.

I have a dream that one day even the state of Mississippi, a state sweltering with the heat of injustice, sweltering with the heat of oppression, will be transformed into an oasis of freedom and justice.

I have a dream that my four little children will one day live in a nation where they will not be judged by the color of their skin but by the content of their character.

I have a dream today! (Dr. Martin Luther King, Jr., I Have a Dream Speech, 1963)

Franklin Delano Roosevelt Memorial

The Franklin Delano Roosevelt Memorial[23] commemorates President Roosevelt's life of public service and leadership during the Great Depression and World War II. Roosevelt's ability to communicate to the citizens of the nation through his "fireside chats" and speeches provided the inspiration and resolve to see the United States through these life changing years of the 1930s and 1940s:

I am certain that my fellow Americans expect that on my induction into the Presidency I will address them with a candor and a decision which the present situation of our people impel. This is preeminently the time to speak the truth, the whole truth, frankly and boldly. Nor need we shrink from honestly facing conditions in our country today. This great Nation will endure as it has endured, will revive and will prosper. So, first of all, let me assert my firm belief that the only thing we have to fear is fear itself—nameless, unreasoning, unjustified terror which paralyzes needed efforts to convert retreat into advance. In every dark hour of our

---

[23] nps.gov/frde/index.htm

178 • **Historic Places of our Republic**

national life a leadership of frankness and vigor has met with that understanding and support of the people themselves which is essential to victory. I am convinced that you will again give that support to leadership in these critical days . . . (Franklin Delano Roosevelt, First Inaugural Address, 1933)

United States Constitution Gardens and 56 Signers Memorial

The United States Constitution Gardens and the 56 Signers Memorial[24] honor all those brave individuals who signed the Declaration of Independence and those who created our Republic, the representative democracy that continues to this moment. The Constitution Gardens were dedicated in 1976 as part of the bicentennial celebration. In 1986, President Reagan issued a proclamation that the gardens are a "living legacy" to honor the Constitution.

We the People of the United States, in Order to form a more perfect Union, establish Justice, insure domestic Tranquility, provide for the common defense, promote the general Welfare, and secure the Blessings of Liberty to ourselves and our Posterity, do ordain and establish this Constitution for the United States of America. (Preamble to the United States Constitution, 1787)

We, therefore, the Representatives of the United States of America, in General Congress, Assembled, appealing to the Supreme Judge of the world for the rectitude of our intentions, do, in the Name, and by Authority of the good People of these Colonies, solemnly publish and declare, That these united Colonies are, and of Right ought to be Free and

---

[24] nps.gov/COGA/index.htm

Independent States, that they are Absolved from all Allegiance to the British Crown, and that all political connection between them and the State of Great Britain, is and ought to be totally dissolved; and that as Free and Independent States, they have full Power to levy War, conclude Peace, contract Alliances, establish Commerce, and to do all other Acts and Things which Independent States may of right do.–And for the support of this Declaration, with a firm reliance on the protection of Divine Providence, we mutually pledge to each other our Lives, our Fortunes, and our sacred Honor. (Declaration of Independence, 1776)

James Madison Building

The James Madison Building[25] is part of the Library of Congress and is named in honor of Madison for his leadership in the writing of the United States Constitution and the Bill of Rights. He was the fourth president of the United States and a proponent for a library of Congress. These are two quotes that provide a sense of his work for our nation:

What is government itself but the greatest of all reflections on human nature? If men were angels, no government would be necessary. If angels were to govern men, neither external nor internal controls on government would be necessary. (James Madison in The Federalist Papers, Number 51, 1788)

In republics, the great danger is, that the majority may not sufficiently respect the rights of the minority. (James Madison, Virginia Convention speech, 1829)

The memorials to individual citizens and the war memorials

---

[25] loc.gov/loc/walls/madison.html

for the many who served our country convey the message that our country might not have been established or preserved without their contributions at critical times in our nation's founding and the preservation of our Republic. Our nation might never have come to fruition or survived without their strength of personality and commitment to a government of the people.

War Memorials and Arlington National Cemetery

The War Memorials and Arlington National Cemetery[26] acknowledge the ultimate sacrifice given by many citizens of the United States. Other wars and conflicts in our past are not acknowledged on the Mall, but the courage and sacrifice of all these efforts can be felt by visiting the memorials concerning Vietnam,[27] Korea,[28] and World War II.[29] Close by, Arlington National Cemetery contains the earthly remains of soldiers from every war and conflict, beginning with the War for Independence. This is the place where those who were never identified are commemorated with the Tomb of the Unknown Soldier from World War I. Close by are the crypts of unknown soldiers' remains from World War II, Korea, and Vietnam.[30]

The Charters of Freedom

The White House, Capitol, and Supreme Court are the structural symbols of our Republic and adjoin the Mall. The decisions and actions of elected and appointed citizens of the United States in these three historic places have shaped the nation we have today. These decisions and actions in the past,

---

[26] arlingtoncemetery.mil/
[27] nps.gov/vive/index.htm
[28] nps.gov/kowa/index.htm
[29] nps.gov/wwii/learn/historyculture/index.htm
[30] arlingtoncemetery.mil/Explore/Tomb-of-the-Unknown-Soldier

Why is the United States the Nation it is Today? • 181

present, and future are based on the words and the interpretations of those words in the Declaration of Independence, United States Constitution, and the Bill of Rights. The decisions and actions of citizens memorialized on the Mall were all connected in some manner to these Charters, either in their creation or following or even both.

The Declaration of Independence, the United States Constitution and the Bill of Rights define our liberty, the structure of our Republic, and our freedoms. As the capital itself, all the events before the Charters' existence led to their creation and all events after are connected in some manner to these charters.

When you enter the Charters of Freedom Rotunda at the National Archives,[31] ask yourself this question and reflect on all you have seen and read: "Why is the United States the nation it is today?" The answer is the Declaration of Independence, the United States Constitution, and the Bill of Rights. Upon completion of elementary school, every student should know and to a certain extent understand why this is the answer.

Then tour the White House, [32] the Capitol, [33] and the Supreme Court[34] to understand the first three articles of the Constitution and the three branches of government. Finally, visit the Smithsonian Museums[35] and other locations with primary sources including the Library of Congress[36] and other exhibits in the National Archives.[37] All together they reinforce the answer to why the United States is the nation it is today.

All citizens of the United States should visit our nation's

---

[31] archives.gov

[32] whitehouse.gov/1600

[33] nps.gov/nr/travel/wash/dc76.htm

[34] supremecourt.gov

[35] si.edu/museums

[36] loc.gov

[37] archives.gov

capital during their lifetime and tour the memorials and then view the Charters of Freedom. The sequence in the writing of these documents is key to understanding why they were written and the debates that led to their fruition. These debates from the past continue even now and will continue in the future. One of these debates concerns the question, "How much should government be involved in our lives and at what level?" The level is either a local, state, or national focus.

Another key debate is, "Who should have the rights of citizenship and what are the specifics of those rights?" The National Mall itself and the surrounding resources provide the foundational knowledge to begin to understand the details of what happened in the past, in the present, and likely in the future concerning the Charters of Freedom and the ongoing debates I have indicated.

In review, this guide is structured with a guiding framework for the study of the past, the history. The first three categories deal with historic places, developing a cognitive map and geography, and literacy. These steps are the preparation to then continue to the next three which include the actual study of history. The actual study of history includes the decisions and actions of people in the past, the connection of time and sequence of these events, and the primary sources that survive to understand and state a position about those decisions and actions. This framework has provided the route for your students to travel the United States and develop a foundational knowledge about our Republic's history.

The ability for all of us to discover the history of the United States is only possible through the preservation of historical knowledge. The Library of Congress, the National Archives, the surrounding Smithsonian and other museums, and the National Park Service conserve the documents, artifacts, and historic places that connect this knowledge to all citizens of the United

States. These efforts for preservation and conservation of all of this for our nation allows us to understand why the United States is the nation it is today.

Links to Historic Homes of Individuals Honored on the National Mall

Mount Vernon (Washington)	nps.gov/nr/travel/presidents/mount_vernon
Monticello (Jefferson)	nps.gov/nr/travel/presidents/jefferson_monticello
Lincoln Home	nps.gov/liho/index.htm
Martin Luther King, Jr. Home	nps.gov/malu/index.htm
Franklin Roosevelt	nps.gov/hofr/index.htm
George Mason	gunstonhall.org
James Madison	montpelier.org/learn/the-life-of-james-madison

Conclusion

Why do we want students to know the history of the United States of America? Your answer to this question obviously shapes what and how you plan to teach the history of our country. For children, an intrinsic interest in what the world was like before they arrived is debatable but, as I mentioned earlier in this guide, curiosity is intrinsic in all of us. What we become curious about is the variable, and nurturing curiosity in students is the best motivator for all subjects.

Traditional instruction in American history often presents government as one aspect of history instruction and the events in our past as another. If I were to answer the question as to why we teach the history of the United States to students, it would be to understand and value our Republic and the ongoing efforts to reach the lofty ideals expressed in the Charters of Freedom.

To be a citizen in our representative democracy, one needs to have a foundational knowledge as to what has gone on in the past, both heroic and horrible, so that each of us can decide for ourselves what to think and act on based on our understanding of what has transpired in the past. For me, understanding the Charters of Freedom is the core for our foundational knowledge.

186 • **Historic Places of our Republic**

If we teach United States history without this emphasis, the events that are read and discussed seem to have little impact on our lives today. If we connect these events to the Charters, the impact on our lives today becomes apparent.

Given the human condition with all its foibles, honoring the Charters is the ideal and the difficulty. Our Founders brought to this continent the ideas for a new way of life which were idealized in the Charters, but they also brought slavery, the quest for wealth and power, jealousy, and a long list of negative human traits. The history of the United States is the evolving interpretation of the Charters; the ongoing debate is how much government we want in our lives and at what level, and who is a citizen with the right to vote. The debate continues with what those rights are and what the role of the government is in those rights.

"We The People" are the government and we elect fellow citizens to represent us to figure all of this out. When we forget our participatory requirement as citizens and the responsibility to be informed to make judgements about all this, including voting, we are in trouble. The quote from Benjamin Franklin is always appropriate in these discussions. When he was asked, after finishing with the Constitutional Convention, what kind of government we now have, he is reputed to have said, "a republic if you can keep it." The Founders were concerned about the survival of the representative democracy they had put into motion and viewed schools as the way to educate the citizenry about their responsibilities and benefits when the people are the government.

This is why this guide is focused on the National Mall and all the elements that are on or nearby the Mall to inform all of us what has happened in the past. That past includes the time before the writing of the Declaration of Independence, the dire need that prompted the writing of the United States Constitution, and the demands of the ratification debate to see the creation of the

Bill of Rights. Then that same Bill of Rights that was to protect all citizens from the abuses of the newly created federal government would later extend to the abuses of any state government, and the struggles as to who is a citizen and what are the rights of that citizenship.

The last chapter in the guide is a tour of the National Mall with quotes from the people and events memorialized at each location. All these words connect in some manner either in the founding or preservation of the nation to the Charters of Freedom on display in the National Archives. The design of the Mall illustrates that the people are at the center with the branches of government at distinct locations to mirror the separation of powers indicated in the Constitution. The Washington Monument is in the approximate center (offset because of issues with the soil to support the weight) to celebrate that Washington was at the center for the establishment of the nation. The Lincoln Memorial is prominently seen to the west, communicating to all visitors the monumental struggle to end slavery and preserve the Union. After touring the memorials, the visit to the rotunda for the Charters of Freedom solidifies the connection to all the words. Finally, ongoing visits to the Smithsonian Museums and other repositories of knowledge like the Library of Congress clarify the centuries of change in our nation with their vast collections of primary sources, many of these directly connecting to the Charters.

Every year of elementary school, students will visit the National Mall and all that is there with additional instruction as to why all of this is important to their lives today. The use of Google Earth and YouTube, along with traditional written resources, provides 21st century benefits for interest and written knowledge to help students to understand the importance of our representative democracy for their lives today. The technology motivates the curiosity to learn through traditional sources about how the past is part of their present and future as well as the future of the Republic.

To organize these travels to the National Mall and other historic places, the guiding framework provides the structure for teachers to teach and students to learn. I have indicated the types of work to be done related to each category of the framework as well as resources and sources online, in print, or on display.

Finally, I want to advocate that the discovery about our representative democracy should begin in earnest with children in elementary school. There is no better time in their lives to begin traveling to the historic places of our Republic.

Why do we teach United States history to our children and students? The answer you give directs what you will teach, when you will do this, how you will do this, whom you will select for emphasis, and where you will start. This guide provides a perspective to discover the answers to these questions.

References

Allison, L., & Burns, M. (1975). *My Backyard History Book*. Brown Books for Young Readers.

Bell, N. (1982). *The Book of Where, Or How to Be Naturally Geographic*. Little, Brown and Co.

Broton, J. (2012) *A History of the World in 12 Maps*. Penguin Books.

Ellis, R.J. (2005). *To the Flag: The Unlikely History of the Pledge of Allegiance*. University Press of Kansas.

Evans, R.W. (2004). *The Social Studies Wars: What Should We Teach the Children?* Teachers College Press.

Fitch, J.M. (1990). *Historic Preservation: Curatorial Management of the Built World*. University of Virginia Press.

Great Books Foundation. (2000). *The Will of the People: Readings in American Democracy*. Great Books Foundation.

Greene, A.J. (2010, July, August). Making Connections: The Essence of Memory is Linking One Thought to Another. *Scientific American Magazine*, (21,3), 22-25.

Hellstern, G.M., Scott, G.M., & Garrison, S.M. (1998). *The History Student Writer's Manual*. Harcourt Brace.

Hirsch, E.D. (1988). *Cultural Literacy: What Every American Needs to Know*. Vintage.

Hirsch, E.D. (2009). *The Making of Americans: Democracy and Our Schools*. Yale University Press.

Kornblith, G.J., & Lesser, C. (2009). *Teaching American History: Essays Adapted from the Journal of American History, 2001-2007*. Bedford/St. Martins.

Kennon, D.R., & Striner, R. (1987). *Washington Past and Present.* United States Capitol.

Loewen, J.W. (2010). *Teaching What Really Happened.* Teacher College Press.

Marshall, T. (2015). *Prisoners of Geography: Ten Maps That Explain Everything About the World.*

Miller, M. (1999). *Words That Built A Nation.* Stonesong Press.

Schmoker, M. (2011). *Focus: Elevating the Essentials to Radically Improve Student Learning.* American Society for Curriculum Development.

Ward, K. (2006). *History in the Making: An Absorbing Look at How American History has Changed in the Telling over the Last 100 Years.* Kyle Ward.

Resources

Resources include books and links. They are divided into several categories to support instruction at all grade levels of elementary school.

The first listing, A, lists important books and texts for teachers and parents that support the development of the foundational knowledge indicated in this guide. Certain grades will use specific texts but all are essential for your own knowledge development and to facilitate your instruction.

The B listing indicates written material for classroom reading by students or for teachers to read to the class. The organization is either for grades K-2 or grades 3-5 but some overlap may be appropriate, given the reading ability of students. These specific books are a brief sampling of some of the excellent books on people and events in United States history for elementary school-age students.

Links are grouped in certain categories based on use and grade level. Group C includes links for all grades, all the links for the National Mall, and links for a few locations nearby in Washington, D.C. All are managed by the National Park Service. These are used specifically for Chapter 7 but can be referenced for Chapter 2 locations. Some of the links in group D reference these links also but it will be less confusing to go to the next group for your specific grade level.

The second group of links, D, is by grade level and the places are referenced in Chapters 4 and 5. There are links listed for grades 4 and 5 that are connected to eras in United States history that can also be of benefit to teachers at all grades. I highly recommend the link to the main page of the National Park Service and the link to the National Park Foundation Owner's Manual. This is an extensive list of all the historic places and parks managed by the National Park Service and it can be useful in the selection of historic places close to or in your state.

The last group, E, lists specific links to teacher resources at the National Archives, the Library of Congress, and the Smithsonian Institution. I have also provided the main links to the National Constitution Center, Bill Of Rights Institute, We The People, Center for Civic Education, Gilder Lehrman Institute of American History, George Washington's Mount Vernon, and Museum of the American Revolution so that you are aware of these excellent institutions and the resources they offer for instruction.

Resources • 193

Group A

Readings to Facilitate Classroom Work (All Teachers)

A History of US: The First Americans. (1993). Joy Hakim, Oxford University Press. (Note: this is the first of a ten-volume series whose first five volumes provide the necessary background knowledge of U.S. history indicated in this guide.)

Being an American: Exploring the Ideals That Unite Us. (2nd Ed.). (2008). Edited by Veronica Burchard. The Bill of Rights Institute.

The Book of Where, Or How to be Naturally Geographic. (1982). Neill Bell. Little, Brown.

D is for Democracy: A Citizen's Alphabet. (2004). Elissa Grodin. Sleeping Bear Press.

Easy Guide to American History. (2005). Sparknotes (Ed.). Fall River Press.

Make it Work! Maps. The Hands-on Approach to Geography. (1996). Andrew Haslam. World Book, Inc.

Maps and Mapping. (2004). Deborah Chancellor. Kingfisher Publications.

My Backyard History. (1975). David Weitzman. Little, Brown, and Company.

We the People: The Citizen & the Constitution-Level 1-2. (2011). Edited by a National Advisory Committee. The Center for Civic Education.

Who's In Charge: How Governments Make the World Go Round. (2010). A. Cox, D. Locke, F. Star, Editors. D. K. Publishing.

The Will of the People: Readings in American Democracy. (2000). Great Books Foundation.

Words That Built A Nation. (1999). Marilyn Miller. Stonesong Press.

O, Say Can You See? America's Symbols, Landmarks, and Inspiring Words. (2004). Sheila Keenan. Scholastic Inc.

194 • **Historic Places of our Republic**

Group B

Written Materials for Students
and Teachers to Read in Class

Kindergarten Through Grade 2

A is for Abigail: An Almanac of Amazing American Women. (2003). Lynn Cheney. Simon & Schuster.

America Votes. How Our President is Elected. (2003). Linda Granfield. Scholastic Inc.

The American Flag. (2014). Lisa M. Herrington. C. Press/F. Watts Trade.

The Bald Eagle. (2012). Alison Eldridge, Stephen Eldridge. Enslow Elementary.

Can You Find It? America. (2010). Linda Falken. Abrams Books for Young Readers.

Capital! Washington D.C. from A to Z. (2003). Laura Krauss Melmed. Laura Krauss Melmed.

The Flag We Love. (2000). Pam Munoz Ryan. Charlesbridge.

Let's Read About George Washington. (2002). Kimberly Weinberger. Scholastic. There are others titles in the "Let's Read..." series.

The Liberty Bell. (2007). Mary Firestone. Picture Window Books.

Lincoln and Douglass: An American Friendship. (2008). Nikki Giovanni. Henry Hold and Company.

The Lincoln Memorial. (2007). Mary Firestone. Picture Window Books.

The Matchbox Diary. (2013). Paul Fleishman. Candlewick Press.

Mount Rushmore. (2012). Alison Eldridge, Stephen Eldridge. Enslow Elementary.

O, Say Can You See? America's Symbols, Landmarks, and Inspiring Words. (2004). Sheila Keenan.

The Pilgrims of Plymouth. (1996). Marcia Sewall. Aladdin Picture Books.

Places in Time: A New Atlas of American History. (2003). Susan Bucley, Eslepth Leacock. Houghton-Miflin Company.

The Statue of Liberty. (2006). Mary Firestone. Picture Window Books.

Sweet Land of Liberty. (2007). Deborah Hopkinson. Peachtree Publishers.

This is the Dream. (2009). Diane Z. Shore and Jessica Alexander. Amistad.

This Is Me: A Story of Who We Are & Where We Came From. (2016). Jamie Lee Curtis, Laura Cornell. Workman Publishing.

The Washington Monument. (2002). Hal Marcovitz. Mason Crest Publishers.

The White House. (2006). Mary Firestone. Picture Window Books.

Understanding the Declaration of Independence. (2012). Sally Senzell Isaacs. Crabtree Publishing Company.

(Crabtree Publishing Company has published many more suitable publications for young readers.)

Grades 3 Through 5

Atlas of Exploration. (1993). Dinah Starkey. Scholastic Inc.

Coming to America Series: Africans in America 1619-1865. (2003). Kay Melchisedech Olson. Blue Earth Books.
(Other topics include Chinese, French, Greek, Irish, Italian, Russian, Norwegian, Swedish, Danish, and Jewish immigrants.)

196 • **Historic Places of our Republic**

D is for Democracy: A Citizen's Alphabet. (2004). Elissa Grodin. Sleeping Bear Press.

The Family Tree Detective: Cracking the Case of Your Family's History. (1999). Ann Douglas. Firefly Books.

The First Americans: The Story of Where They Came From and Who They Became. (2005). Anthony F. Aveni. Scholastic.

Flag: An American Biography. (2005). Marc Leepson. Thomas Dunne Books.

Fritz Book: George Washington's Breakfast. (1997). Jean Fritz and Paul Galdone. The Putnam & Grosset Group.
(Other topics in this series include the writing of the Constitution and people such as Benjamin Franklin, Christopher Columbus, Patrick Henry, John Hancock, King George, and Paul Revere.)

Full Steam Ahead: The Race to Build. a Transcontinental Railroad. (1996). Rhoda Blumberg. Scholastic Inc.

George Washington: The Man Who Would Not Be King. (1991). Stephen Krensky. Scholastic Inc.

Going To School In History Series: Going to School during the Great Depression. (2001). Kerry A. Graves.
(Other topics in this series include the civil rights movement, the Civil War, pioneer times, and colonial America.)

The Great Ancestor Hunt: The Fun of Finding Out Who You Are. (1989). Lila Perl. Clarion Books.

Happy Birthday 1916-2016: America's National Parks. (2016). Bob Grogg. National Park Service.

If You Lived at the Time of Martin Luther King. (1990). Ellen Levine. Scholastic Inc.
(Other topics in this series include colonial times, living with the Iroquois, sailing on the Mayflower, signing of the Constitution, and name changes at Ellis Island.)

The Journey of the one and only Declaration of Independence. (2010). Judith St. George. Scholastic Inc.

Journey to Ellis Island. How My Father Came to America. (1998). Carol Bierman. Scholastic Inc.

Let Freedom Ring Series: The Women Suffrage Movement, 1848-1920. (2003). Kristin Thoenees Keller. Bridgestone Books.
(Other topics in this series include the wilderness road, the War of 1812, the Trail of Tears, the Mexican War, and the early American Industrial Revolution.)

Lincoln: A Photobiography. (1988). Russell Freedman. Scholastic Inc.

Make It Work! Maps. (1996). Barbara Taylor. Two-Can Publishing Ltd.

Places in Time: A New Atlas of American History. (2001). Elspeth Leacock, Susan Buckley. Houghton-Mifflin.

Remember the Ladies 100 Great American Women. (2001). Cheryl Harness. Harper Collins.

Saving the Liberty Bell. (2005). Megan McDonald. Atheneum Books for Young People.

The Signers: The 56 Stories Behind the Declaration of Independence. (2003). Dennis Brindell Fradin. Scholastic Inc.

Wanted Dead or Alive, The True Story of Harriet Tubman. (1965). Ann McGovern. Scholastic Inc.

Washington, D.C., A Scrapbook. (1999). Laura Lee Benson. Demco Media.

Who's In Charge: How Governments Make the World Go Round. (2010). A. Cox, D. Locke, F. Star, Editors. D. K. Publishing.

Words that Built a Nation. A Young Person's Collection of Historic American Documents. (1999). Marilyn Miller. Scholastic Inc.

198 • **Historic Places of our Republic**

Group C

Links for All Grades

Google Earth	google.com/earth
YouTube	youtube.com
National Park Service	nps.gov

Links for the National Mall

National Mall	nps.gov/nama/index.htm
Washington Monument	nps.gov/wamo/index.htm
Lincoln Memorial	nps.gov/Linc/index.htm
Jefferson Memorial	nps.gov/thje/index.htm
George Mason Memorial	nps.gov/nama/planyourvisit/George-Mason-Memorial
Martin Luther King, Jr. Memorial	nps.gov/mlkm/index.htm
Franklin Delano Roosevelt Memorial	nps.gov/frde/index.htm
Constitution Gardens (Memorial to the 56 Signers)	nps.gov/COGA/index.htm
White House	whitehouse.gov/1600
White House Constitution	whitehouse.gov/1600/constitution
White House Executive Branch	whitehouse.gov/1600/executive-branch
White House Legislative Branch	whitehouse.gov/1600/legislative-branch
White House Judicial Branch	whitehouse.gov/1600/judicial-branch

President's Park (White House)   nps.gov/whho/index.htm

U. S. Capitol   nps.gov/nr/travel/dc76.htm

U. S. Capitol Visitor Center   visitthecapitol.gov

Supreme Court   supremecourt.gov

Korean War Veterans Memorial   nps.gov/kowa/index.htm

Vietnam Veterans Memorial   nps.gov/vive/index.htm

World War II Memorial   nps.gov/wwii/learn/historyculture/index.htm

Arlington National Cemetery   arlingtoncemetery.mil

Theodore Roosevelt Island   nps.gov/this/index.htm

National Archives   archives.gov

Library of Congress   loc.gov

Smithsonian Institution   si.edu

Smithsonian Museums   si.edu/Museums

Links for Some Locations Near the National Mall

Ford's Theatre & Petersen Home   nps.gov/foth/the-petersen-house.htm

Frederick Douglass National Historic Site   nps.gov/frdo/learn/historyculture/people.htm

Arlington House, Robert E. Lee   nps.gov/arho/index.htm

200 • **Historic Places of our Republic**

Group D

Links by Grade Level for
Places Referenced in Chapter 4

Kindergarten

National Mall	nps.gov/nama/index.htm
Washington Monument	nps.gov/wamo/index.htm
Lincoln Memorial	nps.gov/Linc/index.htm
Jefferson Memorial	nps.gov/thje/index.htm
George Mason Memorial	nps.gov/nama/planyourvisit/George-Mason-Memorial
Martin Luther King, Jr. Memorial	nps.gov/mlkm/index.htm
Franklin Delano Roosevelt Memorial	nps.gov/frde/index.htm
Constitution Gardens (Memorial to the 56 Signers)	nps.gov/COGA/index.htm
White House	whitehouse.gov/1600
White House Constitution	whitehouse.gov/1600/constitution
White House Executive Branch	whitehouse.gov/1600/executive-branch
White House Legislative Branch	whitehouse.gov/1600/legislative-branch
White House Judicial Branch	whitehouse.gov/1600/judicial-branch
President's Park (White House)	nps.gov/whho/index.htm
U. S. Capitol	nps.gov/nr/travel/wash/dc76.htm
U. S. Capitol Visitor Center	visitthecapitol.gov

Resources • 201

Supreme Court	supremecourt.gov
Korean War Veterans Memorial	nps.gov/kowa/index.htm
Vietnam Veterans Memorial	nps.gov/vive/index.htm
World War II Memorial	nps.gov/wwii/learn/historyculture/index.htm
Arlington National Cemetery	arlingtoncemetery.mil
Theodore Roosevelt Island	nps.gov/this/index.htm
Independence Hall	nps.gov/inde/index.htm
Ellis Island	nps.gov/elis/index.htm
Statue of Liberty	nps.gov/stli/index.htm
Mount Rushmore	nps.gov/Moru/index.htm
Liberty Bell	nps.gov/inde/learn/historyculture/stories-libertybell.htm

First Grade

National Mall	nps.gov/nama/index.htm
Washington Monument	nps.gov/wamo/index.htm
Lincoln Memorial	nps.gov/Linc/index.htm
Jefferson Memorial	nps.gov/thje/index.htm
George Mason Memorial	nps.gov/nama/planyourvisit/George-Mason-Memorial
Martin Luther King, Jr. Memorial	nps.gov/mlkm/index.htm
Franklin Delano Roosevelt Memorial	nps.gov/frde/index.htm
Constitution Gardens (Memorial to the 56 Signers)	nps.gov/COGA/index.htm
White House	whitehouse.gov/1600

White House Constitution	whitehouse.gov/1600/constitution
White House Executive Branch	whitehouse.gov/1600/executive-branch
White House Legislative Branch	whitehouse.gov/1600/legislative-branch
White House Judicial Branch	whitehouse.gov/1600/judicial-branch
President's Park (White House)	nps.gov/whho/index.htm
U. S. Capitol	nps.gov/nr/travel/wash/dc76.htm
U. S. Capitol Visitor Center	visitthecapitol.gov
Supreme Court	supremecourt.gov
Korean War Veterans Memorial	nps.gov/kowa/index.htm
Vietnam Veterans Memorial	nps.gov/vive/index.htm
World War II Memorial	nps.gov/wwii/learn/historyculture/index.htm
Arlington National Cemetery	arlingtoncemetery.mil
Theodore Roosevelt Island	nps.gov/this/index.htm
Independence Hall	nps.gov/inde/index.htm
Ellis Island	nps.gov/elis/index.htm
Statue of Liberty	nps.gov/stli/index.htm
Mount Rushmore	nps.gov/Moru/index.htm
Liberty Bell	nps.gov/inde/learn/historyculture/stories-libertybell.htm

Second Grade

National Mall	nps.gov/nama/index.htm
Washington Monument	nps.gov/wamo/index.htm
Lincoln Memorial	nps.gov/Linc/index.htm
Jefferson Memorial	nps.gov/thje/index.htm
George Mason Memorial	nps.gov/nama/planyourvisit/George-Mason-Memorial
Martin Luther King, Jr. Memorial	nps.gov/mlkm/index.htm
Franklin Delano Roosevelt Memorial	nps.gov/frde/index.htm
Constitution Gardens (Memorial to the 56 Signers)	nps.gov/COGA/index.htm
White House	whitehouse.gov/1600
White House Constitution	whitehouse.gov/1600/constitution
White House Executive Branch	whitehouse.gov/1600/executive-branch
White House Legislative Branch	whitehouse.gov/1600/legislative-branch
White House Judicial Branch	whitehouse.gov/1600/judicial-branch
President's Park (White House)	nps.gov/whho/index.htm
U. S. Capitol	nps.gov/nr/travel/wash/dc76.htm
U. S. Capitol Visitor Center	visitthecapitol.gov
Supreme Court	supremecourt.gov
Korean War Veterans Memorial	nps.gov/kowa/index.htm
Vietnam Veterans Memorial	nps.gov/vive/index.htm
World War II Memorial	nps.gov/wwii/learn/historyculture/index.htm

Arlington National Cemetery	arlingtoncemetery.mil
Theodore Roosevelt Island	nps.gov/this/index.htm
Independence Hall	nps.gov/inde/index.htm
Ellis Island	nps.gov/elis/index.htm
Statue of Liberty	nps.gov/stli/index.htm
Mount Rushmore	nps.gov/Moru/index.htm
Liberty Bell	nps.gov/inde/learn/ historyculture/stories-libertybell.htm
Mount Vernon (Washington)	nps.gov/nr/travel/ presidents/mount_vernon
Monticello (Jefferson)	nps.gov/nr/travel/presidents/ jefferson_monticello
Lincoln Home	nps.gov/liho/index.htm
Martin Luther King, Jr. Home	nps.gov/malu/index.htm
Frederick Douglass	nps.gov/frdo/index.htm
Franklin Roosevelt	nps.gov/hofr/index.htm
Eleanor Roosevelt	nps.gov/elro/index.htm
Susan B. Anthony	nps.gov/wori/learn/ historyculture/ susan-b-nthony
Abigail Adams	nps.gov/adam/abigaibio.htm

Third Grade

National Mall	nps.gov/nama/index.htm
Washington Monument	nps.gov/wamo/index.htm
White House	whitehouse.gov/1600
White House Constitution	whitehouse.gov/1600/ constitution

White House Executive Branch	whitehouse.gov/1600/executive-branch
White House Legislative Branch	whitehouse.gov/1600/legislative-branch
White House Judicial Branch	whitehouse.gov/1600/judicial-branch
President's Park (White House)	nps.gov/whho/index.htm
U. S. Capitol	nps.gov/nr/travel/wash/dc76.htm
U. S. Capitol Visitor Center	visitthecapitol.gov
Supreme Court	supremecourt.gov
National Archives	archives.gov
Library of Congress	loc.gov
Independence Hall	nps.gov/inde/index.htm
National Museum of the American Indian	nmai.si.edu
National Geographic Human Journey	ngm.nationalgeographic.com/ngm/0603/feature2/map.html
Mesa Verde National Park	nps.gov/meve/index.htm
Chaco Culture National Historic Park	nps.gov/cagr/index.htm
Casa Grande Ruins National Monument	nps.gov/cagr/index.htm
Lewis and Clark National Historic Park	nps.gov/lewi/index.htm
Lewis and Clark's Historic Trail	nps.gov/lecl/index.htm
Nez Perce National Historical Park	nps.gov/nepe/index.htm
Owner's Guide to America's National Parks	nationalparks.org/explore-parks/travel-ideas

206 • Historic Places of our Republic

Fourth and Fifth Grades

The introduction of eras in both grades and the emphasis in fourth grade for state history indicates the need to select historic places within your state or nearby, when possible. The Owner's Guide to America's National Parks and the National Park Service main page provide the locations of national parks and historic places throughout the United States that are managed by the National Park Service. The following links provide a broad perspective of resources throughout the nation.

America's Native People: State Parks

On-A-Slant Mandan Village (ND):

   nps.gov/knri/learn/historyculture/mandan.htm

Cahokia Mounds State Park (IL):

   cahokiamounds.org

Serpent Mound State Park (OH):

   ohiohistory.org/visit/museum-and-site-locator/
   serpent-mound

Three Rivers Petroglyph Site (NM):

   blm.gov/nm/st/en/prog/recreation/las_cruces/
   three_rivers.htm

Valley of Fire State Park (NV):

   parks.nv.gov/parks/valley-of-fire

America's Native People: National Park Service

Chaco Culture National Historical Park (NM):

   nps.gov/chcu/index.htm

Mesa Verde National Park (CO)

   nps.gov/meve/index.htm

Aztec Ruins National Monument (NM)

nps.gov/azru/index.htm

Bandelier National Monument (NM)

nps.gov/Band/index.htm

Gila Cliff Dwellings National Monument (NM)

nps.gov/gicl/index.htm

Walnut Canyon National Monument (AZ)

nps.gov/waca/index.htm

Canyon de Chelly National Monument (AZ)

nps.gov/cach/index.htm

Wupatki National Monument (AZ)

nps.gov/wupa/index.htm

Casa Grande Ruins National Monument (AZ)

nps.gov/cagr/index.htm

National Park Service Links for 4th and 5th Grade

Owner's Guide to America's National Parks	nationalparks.org/ explore-parks/travel-ideas
National Park Service	nps.gov
The Civil War	nps.gov/civilwar/index.htm
The Civil War Parks	nps.gov/cwindepth/ cwparks.htm
The Civil War Places	nps.gov/civilwar/places.htm
Sites of Remembrance (Civil War, Revolutionary War, etc)	nps.gov/planyourvisit/ military-remember.htm

208 • **Historic Places of our Republic**

Industrial Revolution in England (Lowell, MA):

nps.gov/lowe/learn/photosmultimedia/Industry.htm

American Industrial Revolution:

nps.gov/pagr/learn/historyculture/the-birthplace-of-the-american-industrial-revolution.htm

Birthplace of the American Industrial Revolution (MA and RI):

nps.gov/blac/learn/historyculture/index.htm

Teaching With Historic Places

nps.gov/subjects/teachingwithhistoricplaces/index.htm

Boott Cotton Mills (Losell, MA)

nps.gov/nr/twhp/wwwlps/lessons/21boott/21boott.htm

The American Revolution

nps.gov/revwar

Westward Expansion: Jefferson National Expansion Memorial

nps.gov/jeff/index.htm

Decades of Western Expansion, The 1850s

nps.gov/jeff/learn/historyculture/upload/decades_of_westward_expansion.pdf

Westward Expansion

nps.gov/jotr/learn/education/upload/unitX_WestwardExpansion.pdf

The War and Westward Expansion

nps.gov/articles/the-war-and-westward-expansion.html

The War and Westward Movement (Civil War)

nps.gov/civilwar/war-and-westward-movement.htm

Exodusters (black migration, Black Exodus)

nps.gov/home/learn/historyculture/exodusters.htm

America's Diverse Cultural Heritage

nps.gov/nr/travel/cultural_diversity/Preserving_the_Places_
and_Stories_of_Americas_Diverse_Cultural
%20Heritage.html

Discover History

nps.gov/history/index.htm

Native American Heritage

nps.gov/americanindian

Places Reflecting America's Diverse Cultures

nps.gov/nr/travel/cultural_diversity/list_of_sites.html

Working with Native Americans

nps.gov/history/tribes

Don't forget the "Discovering Your Own Community" lesson plan as
well as others for your grade level on http://honoringtriballegacies.com
(This is not a paid site, even though it is a dot com. It is from the
National Park Service.)

The NPS National Mall App:

nps.gov/nama/learn/news/national-mall-and-memorial-parks-
app.htm

210   •   **Historic Places of our Republic**

Group E

Institutions with Teacher Resources

This group lists links specific to teacher resources at the National Archives, the Library of Congress, and the Smithsonian Institution. I have also provided the main links to the National Constitution Center, Bill Of Rights Institute, We The People, Center for Civic Education, Gilder Lehrman Institute of American History, George Washington's Mount Vernon, and the Museum of the American Revolution.

Smithsonian Institution Teacher Resources

The Smithsonian Center for Learning and Digital Access created the Smithsonian Learning Lab to inspire the discovery and creative use of its rich digital materials—more than a million images, recordings, and texts. It is easy to find something of interest because search results display pictures rather than lists. Whether you've found what you were looking for or just discovered something new, it's easy to personalize it. Add your own notes and tags, incorporate discussion questions, and save and share. The Learning Lab makes it simple.

Short animations to get started:
learninglab.si.edu/discover
learninglab.si.edu/create
learninglab.si.edu/share

For K-5 history educators, the Learning Lab allows them (and their students) to utilize rich primary and secondary source material, ranging from artworks, artifacts, illustrations, photographs, postage stamps, and other digital media to explore content in depth first-hand. Using Learning Lab tools, such as text annotations, hotspots, and quiz questions, teachers can adapt the reading level of museum label text, direct students to take note of specific details of an image and assess their understanding before moving on to other content. Students can also use the digitized collections of the museum to create their own collections demonstrating their own research and content knowledge. Additional Resources for Children in grades K through 4:

americanhistory.si.edu/ourstory

Other resources appropriate for elementary level:

historyexplorer.si.edu

National Archives Teacher Resources

Archives Education homepage: archives.gov/education
Docs Teach: docsteach.org
Document Analysis: archives.gov/education/
lessons/worksheets
History Pin: archives.gov/social-media/
historypin.html
Educators' Blog: education.blogs.archives.gov

Teachers should go to docsteach.org (this is the National Archives' main online resource for teachers). Go there and see what wonderful resources are available! archives.gov/education is the best starting place for educational materials. You can get to DocsTeach from there as well as Distance Learning and the Education Updates blog.

Library of Congress Teacher Resources

The Library of Congress Magazine—Back to School issue contains a great deal of information about programs and resources for teachers:

loc.gov/lcm/pdf/LCM_2013_0910.pdf

"Kindergarten Historians" Blog post:

blogs.loc.gov/teachers/2013/03/kindergarten-historians-primary-sources-in-an-early-elementary-classroom

212 • **Historic Places of our Republic**

Curriculum materials and professional development:

loc.gov/teachers

Teaching with the Library of Congress:

blogs.loc.gov/teachers/

Department of Education's online newsletter. Sign up at:

public.govdelivery.com/accounts/USED/subscriber/
new?topic_id=USED_34

The National Mall project developed by the GMU Center for History
and New Media:

chnm.gmu.edu/histories-of-the-national-mall

Additional Organizations with Teacher Resources

National Constitution Center:
constitutioncenter.org

Bill of Rights Institute:
billofrightsinstitute.org

We The People, Center for Civic Education:
civiced.org/programs/wtp

Gilder Lehrman Institute of American History:
gilderlehrman.org

George Washington's Mount Vernon
mountvernon.org/education/for-teachers/

Museum of the American Revolution
amrevmuseum.org/

iCivics
icivics.org

Index

analysis skills, 93–94
Anderson, Marian, 175
archeology, 159–160
architecture, 160–161
Arlington National Cemetery, 180
assessments, 99, 107
attention spans, 38, 95

Bill of Rights, 173, 175–176. *See also* Charters of Freedom
Boston, Massachusetts, 84
Bradley Commission on History in Schools, 90
Bretton, J., 18
buildings
  historic homes, 47, 75, 183
  as local history, 160–161
  one-room schools, 75–76

California content standards. *See also* standards
  analysis skills, 93–94
  as baseline, 89–90
  fifth grade, 136
  first grade, 103–104
  fourth grade, 128
  kindergarten, 96
  second grade, 111
  third grade, 120–121
capitalism, 75, 81
Capitol. *See* U.S. Capitol Building; Washington, D.C.
Casa Grande Ruins (Arizona), 155
cemeteries, 158–159
Center for Civic Education, 121
Charters of Freedom
  in fifth grade curriculum, 137
  historical eras and, 80
  historic places and, 36, 38, 39

student understanding of, 77–78, 83–84
"why" question and, 180–182, 185–187
chronological thinking, 93–94
Civil War, 55, 81, 85, 156
cognitive map
  curriculum overview, 49–50
  fifth grade curriculum, 85, 138–139
  first grade curriculum, 105–106
  fourth grade curriculum, 82–83, 130
  in guiding framework, 17–19, 23
  kindergarten curriculum, 97–98
  learning and, 37, 73
  National Mall example, 43
  second grade curriculum, 112–113
  third grade curriculum, 123–124
Cold War, 81, 156
colonization, 48, 79, 155–156
concept, defined, 90
conflicts and injustices, 55, 75, 77
consciousness, dual, 16, 41
Constitution. *See* Charters of Freedom
Constitution Gardens, 178–179
content standards. *See* California content standards; standards
curiosity, 11, 27, 38, 92
current events, 84
curriculum. *See also specific grade levels or subject matter*
  defined, 61–62, 69, 90
  designing, 69–70
  "Expanding Horizons," 63, 90, 146
  reference for, 63

213

214 • **Historic Places of our Republic**

curriculum *(continued)*
   sequence issue in, 64–65, 66, 73
   spiral, 70
   use throughout the grades, 71–72

decisions and actions
   change and, 56–57
   in family history, 147
   fifth grade curriculum, 140–141
   first grade curriculum, 107–108
   fourth grade curriculum, 132–133
   in guiding framework, 23–26
   kindergarten curriculum, 100
   National Mall example, 44–45
   second grade curriculum, 114–115
   third grade curriculum, 125–126
Declaration of Independence. *See*
   Charters of Freedom;
   Constitution Gardens
Department of the Interior, 15–16

education
   anthropological view, 21
   elementary-school, 93, 119
   history priority in, 53
   mission of, 16–17
Ellis, R., 56
Ellis Island, 38
eras. *See* historical eras
Evans, R.W., 23–24
Executive Branch, 45
"Expanding Horizons," 63, 90, 146

Facebook, 148
family history, 146–148
Farewell Address (Washington),
   169–171
Federal Hall, 38, 84
field trips, 12, 149–150, 152–153,
   157–159
fifth grade

California standards, 136
cognitive map curriculum, 49,
   85, 138–139
decisions and actions curriculum,
   140–141
foundational knowledge, 83–86
geography skills curriculum, 49,
   138–139
historian work in, 162–163
historic places curriculum, 48,
   137–138
literacy curriculum, 139–140
Pledge of Allegiance lessons, 54,
   56
primary sources curriculum, 142
recommended reading for, 143
time and eras curriculum, 48, 58,
   66, 136–137, 141–142
travelogue, 139–140
56 Signers Memorial, 178–179
The First Americans (Hakim), 121
first grade
   California standards, 103–104
   cognitive map curriculum, 49,
   105–106
   decisions and actions curriculum,
   107–108
   foundational knowledge, 74–75
   geography skills curriculum,
   105–106
   historic places curriculum, 47,
   104–105
   literacy curriculum, 106–107
   literacy vocabulary, 44
   Pledge of Allegiance lessons, 54
   primary sources curriculum, 109
   recommended reading for, 110
   symbol and landmark lessons,
   39–40, 99
   time curriculum, 108
   travelogue, 106–107
Fitch, James Marston, 16–17, 41
Focus (Schmoker), 86
Fort McHenry, 38

foundational knowledge
  fifth grade, 83–86
  first grade, 74–75
  fourth grade, 79–83
  kindergarten, 74–75
  second grade, 75–77
  third grade, 77–79
fourth grade
  California standards, 128
  cognitive map curriculum, 49,
    82–83, 130
  decisions and actions curriculum,
    132–133
  foundational knowledge, 79–83
  geography skills curriculum, 49,
    82–83, 130
  historian work in, 162–163
  historic places curriculum, 48,
    129–130
  literacy curriculum, 131–132
  Pledge of Allegiance lessons, 54,
    56
  primary sources curriculum,
    134–135
  recommended reading for, 135
  time and eras curriculum, 58,
    79–83, 133, 135, 154
  travelogue, 131–132
  world history in, 151
framework, defined, 90
Franklin, Ben, 186
Franklin Delano Roosevelt
  Memorial, 36, 177–178
freedom, 73
Freedom Trail, 84

Gadsden Purchase, 156
Garrison, S.M., 24
geography (discipline), 24, 68, 149,
  151–152
geography skills
  curriculum overview, 49–50
  fifth grade curriculum, 138–139
  first grade curriculum, 105–106

foundational knowledge, 74–75
fourth grade curriculum, 82–83,
  130
in guiding framework, 17–19, 23
kindergarten curriculum, 97–98
map making, map use, 42, 43–
  44, 49, 149
second grade curriculum, 112–
  113
third grade curriculum, 123–124
George Mason Memorial, 172–173
gestalt, 14
Gettysburg Address, 173–174
Gilder Lehrman Institute of
  American History, 82, 85,
  153–154
goal, defined, 90
Google Earth
  benefits of, 29–30, 40
  for cognitive mapping, 50
  National Mall visit, 35, 42
government branches
  in third grade curriculum, 48
  visual proof of, 34, 36
Great Books Foundation, 168
Great Depression, 81, 156, 157–158
Greene, A.J., 69
guiding framework. *See also specific*
  categories
  for National Mall lessons, 41–47
  overview, 13–14, 32
  preparatory categories, 14, 15–23
  study of history categories, 14,
    23–30

Hakim, Joy, 121
Hellstern, G.M., 24
Hirsch, E.D., Jr., 16–17, 20, 21
historians, 161–163
historical eras
  in fifth grade curriculum, 48, 66,
    136–137
  in fourth grade curriculum, 79–
    83, 135, 154

216 • **Historic Places of our Republic**

historical eras *(continued)*
Gilder Lehrman perspective, 153–154
local history and, 154–159
historical interpretation, 94
historic places. *See also specific places*
curriculum overview, 47–48
fifth grade curriculum, 137–138
first grade curriculum, 104–105
fourth grade curriculum, 129–130
in guiding framework, 15–17, 23
in-person visits to, 149–150
kindergarten curriculum, 96–97
second grade curriculum, 111–112
third grade curriculum, 122
virtual visits to, 29–30, 40, 73
Historic Preservation (Fitch), 16, 41
historic preservation guidelines, 15–16
history
approach to teaching, 25–26
changing views of, 24–25
low priority in education, 53
as social science, 23–25, 64
history of human decisions and actions. *See* decisions and actions
A History of the U.S. (Hakim), 121
A History of the World in 12 Maps (Bretton), 18
holidays, lessons from, 65
homes, historic, 47, 75, 183
human migration, 48, 67–68, 77, 151

"I Have a Dream" (King), 29, 175, 176–177
immigration, 55
Independence Hall, 38, 84, 159–160
Industrial Revolution, 81

James Madison Building, 179–180
Jefferson, Thomas, 172
Jefferson Memorial, 36, 172
justice. *See* conflicts and injustices

Keenan, Sheila A., 39, 44
Kennon, D.R., 34, 166
kindergarten
California standards, 96
cognitive map curriculum, 49, 97–98
decisions and actions curriculum, 100
foundational knowledge, 74–75
geography skills curriculum, 97–98
historic places curriculum, 47, 96–97
literacy curriculum, 98–99
Pledge of Allegiance lessons, 54
primary sources curriculum, 101–103
recommended reading for, 103
symbol and landmark lessons, 39–40, 99
time curriculum, 101
travelogue, 98–99
King, Martin Luther, Jr., 29, 36, 175, 176–177
Korean War, 81
Kornblith, G.J., 25

Lasser, C., 25
lesson plans, defined, 63
Lincoln, Abraham, 173–176
Lincoln Memorial, 35, 173–176
literacy
curriculum overview, 50–52
defined, 20, 69
fifth grade curriculum, 139–140
first grade curriculum, 106–107
foundational knowledge, 74
fourth grade curriculum, 131–132

Index • 217

literacy *(continued)*
  in guiding framework, 20–23
  kindergarten curriculum, 98–99
  National Mall and, 44, 167–168
  Pledge of Allegiance and, 52–56
  second grade curriculum, 113–114
  successful learning and, 93
  third grade curriculum, 124–125
literacy standards, 62–63
local history
  buildings as, 160–161
  in cemeteries, 158–159
  family history as, 146–148
  field trips, 149–150, 152–153, 157–159
  historical eras and, 154–159
  introducing concept of, 78
  state history as, 79–80
  world history and, 150–152
Loewen, J.W., 28–29, 145–146, 147–148, 162–163, 168

Madison, James, 179–180
Manifest Destiny, 54, 80, 156
map making, map use, 42, 43–44, 49, 149
Marshall, T., 18
Martin Luther King, Jr. (MLK) Memorial, 36, 176–177
Mason, George, 172–173
memorization, vs. understanding, 19, 65, 76, 83, 92–93
memory, 69
Miller, M., 167–168
museums, on National Mall, 36, 46, 79

national anthem, 38, 76
National Geographic, 67
nationalism, vs. patriotism, 168
National Mall
  grade-level lessons, 39–40
  guiding framework for, 41–47

  introducing history with, 35, 74
  as key to teaching, 41, 72–73
  virtual visits to, 35–37, 42, 47
  visitor enthusiasm, 34–35
  "why" questions and, 165–167
national monuments and
    memorials. *See also* Charters
    of Freedom
  Arlington National Cemetery, 180
  Constitution Gardens, 178–179
  George Mason Memorial, 172–173
  James Madison Building, 179–180
  Jefferson Memorial, 36, 172
  Lincoln Memorial, 173–176
  MLK Memorial, 176–177
  Roosevelt Memorial, 36, 177–178
  war memorials, 180
  Washington Monument, 35, 40–41, 43, 45, 169–172
National Park Service, 15–16, 35, 45, 152
National Register of Historic Places, 152, 161
national symbols, landmarks
  content standards and, 38
  grade-level lessons, 39–40, 99
native peoples, 48, 78–79
New York City, 38, 84
911 Memorial, 38

O, Say Can You See (Keenan), 39, 44
online resources
  balanced use of, 29
  frustrations with, 46
  for National Mall lessons, 45
  present perspective and, 73
  as primary sources, 29–30
organization, need for, 11

past, relating to, 26–27, 59

patriotism, vs. nationalism, 168
Philadelphia, Pennsylvania, 38, 84,
   159–160
Pledge of Allegiance, 52–56, 76
prehistoric sites, 48, 155
present perspective, 27, 33, 73, 153
primary resources, 58
primary sources
   defined, 58
   fifth grade curriculum, 142
   first grade curriculum, 109
   fourth grade curriculum, 134–
      135
   in guiding framework, 28–30,
      64–65
   introduction to, 39, 148
   kindergarten curriculum, 101–
      103
   for National Mall lessons, 46
   second grade curriculum, 76,
      116–117
   third grade curriculum, 127
Progressive Movement, 81

questions. *See* Socratic approach;
   "why" questions

reading
   literacy and, 20–21
   to students, 39, 44–45, 93
religious freedom, 55
Republic
   citizen representation in, 78
   state government as, 145
   visual representations of, 34, 36–
      37
   vocabulary development and, 55,
      56
research projects, 76, 79, 85
research skills, 94
Roosevelt, Franklin D., 157–158,
   177–178
Roosevelt memorial, 36, 177–178
"rule of three," 13

"Rules of Civility" (Washington),
   46
Schmoker, Mike, 86
schools, one-room, 75–76
Scott, G.M., 24
secondary sources, 28, 65
second grade
   California standards, 111
   cognitive map curriculum, 112–
      113
   decisions and actions curriculum,
      114–115
   foundational knowledge, 75–77
   geography skills curriculum,
      112–113
   historic places curriculum, 47,
      111–112
   literacy curriculum, 113–114
   primary sources curriculum, 76,
      116–117
   recommended reading for, 117
   symbol and landmark lessons, 40
   time curriculum, 115–116
   travelogue, 113–114
sequence of content presentation,
   23, 64–65, 66, 73
sequence time lines, 57–58, 64, 82,
   85, 135
shared inquiry, 168
sidewalks, 157–158
slavery, 81, 84, 173
social sciences, 23–25, 64
Socratic approach, 50–51
spatial thinking, 93–94
spiraling, 70
standards. *See also* California
   content standards;
   foundational knowledge
   defined, 38, 61–62, 69, 90–91
   national symbols, landmarks
      and, 38
   reference for, 63
   state-specific, 89, 91
   types of, 62–63

Star-Spangled Banner, 38, 76
state history, 48, 79–80, 81–82, 145
Supreme Court Building, 36

teaching
    attention spans and, 38, 95
    guiding framework overview,
        13–14, 32
    information coverage in, 37–38,
        65
    spiraling approach, 70
technology. *See* online resources
third grade
    California standards, 120–121
    cognitive map curriculum, 49,
        123–124
    decisions and actions curriculum,
        125–126
    foundational knowledge, 77–79
    geography skills curriculum,
        123–124
    historic places curriculum, 47–
        48, 122
    literacy curriculum, 124–125
    primary sources curriculum, 127
    recommended reading for, 128
    symbol and landmark lessons, 40
    time curriculum, 126
    travelogue, 124–125
    world history in, 151
time. *See also* historical eras
    fifth grade curriculum, 58, 141–
        142
    first grade curriculum, 108
    fourth grade curriculum, 58, 133
    in guiding framework, 26–27
    kindergarten curriculum, 101
    perspective and complexity of,
        57–58
    present perspective, 27, 33, 73,
        153
    second grade curriculum, 115–
        116
    third grade curriculum, 126

time lines. *See* sequence time lines
travelogue
    archives of, 22, 52, 73–74
    as assessment medium, 99, 107
    fifth grade, 139–140
    first grade, 106–107
    fourth grade, 131–132
    in guiding framework, 22–23
    kindergarten, 98–99
    National Mall example, 43, 44
    second grade, 113–114
    third grade, 124–125
Tucson, Arizona, 155–156

United States Constitution. *See*
        Charters of Freedom
United States Constitution
        Gardens, 178–179
United States flag, 38–39, 54
U.S. Capitol Building, 36

vocabulary development
    National Mall example, 44
    with Pledge of Allegiance, 53–56
    Socratic approach, 50–51

walking tours, 161
Walk the World Project, 67
Ward, K., 25
Ward, W.A., 27
war memorials, 180
Washington, D.C., 33–34. *See also*
        National Mall; national
        monuments and memorials
Washington, George
    Farewell Address, 169–171
    Federal Hall and, 38
    as founding father, 41, 43, 169
    primary sources for, 46
    relating to past and, 26–27
    standards set by, 45–46
    study of, 44
Washington Monument
    online resources for, 45

220 • Historic Places of our Republic

Washington Monument *(continued)*
  visits to, 35, 40–41, 43
  "why question" and, 169–172
westward expansion, 54, 80–81, 156
We the People series (Center for
    Civic Education), 121
"where" questions, 51
White House, 36
"why" questions
  Arlington National Cemetery
      and, 180
  Charters of Freedom and, 180–
      182, 185–187
  Constitution Gardens and, 178–
      179
  curriculum sequence and, 64–65
  George Mason Memorial and,
      172–173
  in historians' work, 161–163
  James Madison Building and,
      179–180
  Jefferson Memorial and, 172
  as key to learning and literacy,
      51, 165

Lincoln Memorial and, 173–176
MLK Memorial and, 176–177
National Mall and, 165–167
Roosevelt memorial and, 177–
    178
war memorials and, 180
Washington Monument and,
    169–172
The Will of the People (Great Books
    Foundation), 168
Works Progress Administration
    (WPA), 157
world geography, 77
world history, 66–69, 150–152
World Wars, 81, 156
WPA (Works Progress
    Administration), 157

YouTube
  for cognitive mapping, 50
  as primary resource, 29, 45

Acknowledgements

I want to thank Elaine Owens for her significant assistance in the completion of this book.

A special thanks also to Dr. Kendra Gaines for her editing and review throughout the process, and to Phyllis MacDonald and Bonnie Darby for their introspective comments.

This book would not have happened without the creative and invaluable design work of Richard Fenwick and Lori Lieber.

About the Author

This guide is based on my decades of teaching, advocacy for historic preservation, and work as a guide of historic districts in Tucson, Arizona. I have spent many summer vacations traveling to historic places around the United States, most preserved and interpreted by the National Park Service. As a civic-minded adult, I take part in city council meetings and attend town halls held by our local, state, and national representatives. I write guest editorials in our local newspaper, and participate in peaceful protests. I consider my interest in history a contributing factor to being an active participant in our republic.

Ken Scoville

onehistoryguy@gmail.com

Made in the USA
Lexington, KY
25 February 2018